All In a Day's Work

Volume 1

MIKE DIXON

ISBN: 978-1-960764-09-6 (sc)
ISBN: 978-1-960764-10-2 (hc)
ISBN: 978-1-960764-11-9 (eBook)

Write and Release
PUBLISHING

www.writeandreleasepublishing.com

Table of Contents

Love Will Always Find Its Way Home

"You there! Get the hell away from here! You filthy bum! Every day you come here to beg, to steal, to stench up my market and run my customers off. I'll call the police. They'll find a place for you all right. Someone will find your body at the bottom of the river. Now be gone! Off with you!"

And with that, poor Alexi Symyonovich peered up at Malechak, the store owner, with guilty, swollen eyes. He was in a state of disdain, shock, and disbelief. And no matter how bad he had wanted to snap back at Malechak, he knew it was no use. After all, Malechak was right. He WAS a bum! He was nothing more than a rotten beggar. Alexi turned, head bowed, and began to shuffle along Karensky Street toward Karkov Park, two kilometers away.

He walked hunched over, his forty-year-old, arthritic body bruised and callous from living like an animal. He wore old tattered brown pants that hung loose around his hips, an old red flannel shirt, and a pair of oversized work boots he had taken off from a corpse that he had stumbled upon the night before by the river.

As he walked, he stared down at the soggy, dirt path that led to the edge of the town square and onto the outskirts of Karkov Park. He looked at his hands, holding an old satchel containing his writings. His hands were black with soot from scraps of coal at the train station the night before. He brushed back his now long, oily, and vile-smelling hair. He began to tremble from the night's cold and he folded his short, stocky arms across his chest as if seeking some false warmth from the bitter cold that was filling the evening air.

Alexi made his way to the park and turned right at the familiar old spruce tree with the three protruding branches that "looked like a pitch fork." He descended down an embankment that led to the Vodski River. Several meters from the water's edge, he suddenly halted and turned his head from side to side as if surveying the area and making sure he hadn't been seen or followed. Next, he reached down and grasped what looked like a handful or clump of leaves and branches, but was actually a "cover" he had made from cloth, leaves, sticks, and grass. He lifted it up only to reveal a hole dug out at the base of a large oak tree. The hole was just large enough for him to crouch his five-foot frame into and curl up. Once settled, he pulled his "roof" over his head and gazed up at the heavens through a small opening he had made with his index finger. He looked at the brightest star in the sky and began to reminisce.

"What happened? I was on the verge of being a great author. I had a beautiful wife, Anastasia, a wonderful, most precious daughter, Natasha. I had a dacha on the banks of the Neva River. I was making 50 rubles a week as an editor of a highly regarded state newspaper. Buy why? They drained me. Set me insane. And for this devotion I lost my wife and my most irreplaceable ruby—my dear Natasha! Oh how I long to see you again…"

Alexi's eyes began to close. His hands became numb from the cold, and he started to shake uncontrollably. And finally, as he had done each night for the last fifteen years, he sobbed himself to sleep. And as he did, he began to dream the same dream he always had, "You promised, Anastasia. You swore to me that you would never leave! I have given everything to you, to Natasha, and to everyone. Why?"

But one day in the spring, Anastasia did leave him, taking ten-year-old Natasha with her as well. The small dacha, the garden, and the counting of Kopecks was all too demeaning to her. So, on one fateful day in May, she revealed to him that she had been having an affair with one government attorney, Konstantin Vladirovich Akmatovich, and that she and Natasha were leaving with the honorable and wealthy gentleman to his estate in Riga.

Things began to go bad for Alexi the right way. The government closed the newspaper and the censors refused his latest novel. He could not find work, but for menial tasks, and without spirit he could no longer write. Soon, he gathered his writings, put them in his satchel, and left the banks of the Neva and headed south. Some two months later, after wandering for hundreds of kilometers he arrived at Karkou Park in the city of Gorodok. There he laid claim to his oak tree and hollowed out his home. And for the past fifteen years, he has roamed the streets of Gorodok as a "madman," a "drunkard," "a heathen."

"Good morning, Mrs. Lubounaya! How are you?"

"Fine, Alexi. And where is the great writer off to today?"

"Why am I off to see the provincial governor himself? He has requested my presence to begin writing his memoirs at once."

"Ha! Alexi! You're entertaining. Are you writing?" "Oh, yes! I've just completed six more poems, two short stories, and I am about finished with a beautiful love story. It's about a little girl and her father. They would play together in the tall grass around their dacha. They would gather mushrooms, sing songs, and he would put her to sleep at night by telling her stories. And the man's wife was…"

"Alexi! That's dandy! Now, my kiosk is dirty. Tidy it up please; straighten my goods on the shelves, dump the trash, get your cup of tea and bread, and be gone please. I've no time for novels about little girls and their daddies. Now hurry, the train will soon be here and I'll have a hundred customers. Lord knows you'd scare them off. Now please hurry."

"Yes, Mrs. Lubounaya. Thank you, ma'am."

And, Alexi, his heart heavy and with tears in his eyes, finished his tasks, drank his tea, ate his stale bread, and departed. A young doctor had been reading the newspaper and sipping on black tea when he couldn't help overhearing Alexi and Mrs. Lubounaya speaking. He turned to the lady and remarked, "Sad, isn't it. Poor fellow."

"Yes," Mrs. L. began sadly and softly. "Yes, it's a shame. Tells me the same story every day, as if it were real or something. Poor fellow indeed. To have a dream only to see it vanish."

"I wonder who he really is," asked the doctor.

"No telling. He's come here every day for fifteen years. Always carries that damn old satchel with him. Won't show it to anyone but says he has the makings of Tolstoy and Chekhov in it. Poor thing. This homelessness can lead to these conditions I suppose. But the daughter part must be true. He shows everyone a picture of a beautiful little brown-eyed girl. He carries on about her, pretends he's talking to her. It's a terribly sad thing to watch." Alexi had reached the center of Gorodok and had started down a narrow cobblestone path that led to the governor's mansion. As he walked, he began to talk to himself about his daughter, Natasha. Soon, he was walking faster and faster until he broke into a run, and all the while, he gripped his satchel to his chest. Soon, he arrived at a large brick and stone building. Standing outside two large oak doors were two royal guards. Alexi approached confidently and exclaimed, "Good day, gentlemen! I have an appointment with the governor. I am to begin the Lordship's memoirs at once. Please be so kind as to announce my presence. I am Alexi Symyonovich of Gorodok. I…" "Take another step and we'll pummel you!", one of the guards snapped.

Alexi kept approaching. Suddenly the two burly guards struck Alexi in the head with their rifle butts, sending him to the ground in a heap. Slowly he got up, looked up in a dumbfounded state, and staggered backward, then finally fell down the steps. He got up clutching his bloody skull with one hand and picked up his satchel with the other, which had fallen, and began to tumble toward Karkov Park. Once in his dwelling, he lay motionless, staring up at the stars.

Finally, he passed out.

Two days later Alexi awoke. His head hurt and he was more saddened than ever before. Holding his satchel to his chest, he weaved his way to the river's bank and sat down. He opened his satchel and took out a handful of crumpled papers. He began to read aloud, "And once again, wild flowers bloomed, children sang happy songs, and the black birds flew freely once more. The sun was crimson, the moon and stars so bright. The father and his daughter were reunited and…"

Alexi began to weep again. He lay down and, holding on to this page, he fell into a deep sleep again.

Meanwhile, a carriage had arrived at the police station in town. A young, beautiful woman of twenty-five exited the coach accompanied by a handsome captain.

"May I help you," the police chief inquired.

"Yes, my name is Natasha Symyonovich. I am looking for my father, the author, Peter Symyonovich. It is reported that he journeyed here some years ago."

"You mean Alexi?"

"Yes! That is his nickname."

"The man in rags that carries an old satchel and speaks of writing novels? This man is your father?"

"Oh yes, your lordship! Where can he be found?"

"In Karkov Park, by the river's edge. He lives underneath an oak tree. He's mad!"

Natasha and the captain climbed in the coach and ordered the driver to whip up the horses and head for Karkov Park. They arrived some two hours later. Natasha got out, followed by the captain. Both ran down the path until they came to the oak tree. Farther down on the water's edge, lay Alexi.

"Papa! Papa!" Natasha cried out.

"Papa! It's me! NATASHA!"

Alexi lay motionless, too weak to move. But his eyes went wide open at the sound of the young woman's voice. Natasha approached slowly and quietly. She knelt next to her father, held his hand, and lay his head in the palm of her other hand. She could see the "novel" in Alexi's grasp. She reached to take it from him.

Just then Alexi turned his head and saw Natasha's big, beautiful brown eyes. They both froze as their eyes met. Then, Alexi whispered meekly, "Natasha. My sweet Natasha."

Natasha leaned forward and kissed her father on the forehead. The young captain looked on with tears of joy. Then Natasha rested Alexi's head in her lap and took the paper Alexi was holding. She began to read aloud, "The father and his daughter were reunited and the pain and suffering all but vanished..."

And as Natasha stared into her father's distant eyes, she read the last line of the novel from memory—something Alexi had always told Natasha as a little girl:

"LOVE WILL ALWAYS FIND ITS WAY HOME."

Jan. 27, 1995

An Author's Agony—Ended

"You there! Old man! Get the hell off my porch! This is private property. I'll call the Ministry of Law himself if you keep this up. Now away with you!"

And with that, the gray-haired, hunched-over, seventy-three-year-old Konstantin looked the proprietor meekly yet coldly in the eye and responded, "But, sir, I am Konstantin Bezuchken, famous Russian author. Look, I have them here. All that you requested, the twenty short stories, the three novels, the book of poetry. My God, Valentin, don't you remember our contract? It was only yesterday that we agreed. You must remember the 100,000 ruble agreement we made? Why, we sipped vodka until the sun rose above the banks of the Neva. Come Valentin! I can't believe for a second that..."

"Off with you! You crazy fool! You're a lunatic. You belong in Yazganny Hospital. That's it! I'm calling the police! This instant!" Konstantin was frightened, turned around, and, moving with a limp, shuffled off down the street to Akady Park. Once there, he found his favorite spot underneath a birch tree. He piled the stacks of leaves around him, threw his yak-skin coat over his shoulders, and lay down on the damp, black soil that was his bed. Akady Park was his home.

The police arrived at Valentin Chenka's residence, 209 Pladovodsky Street, shortly after 2:00 a.m. The watch commander,

Victor Semashkon, had been summoned to make the call himself. Annoyed, he demanded of Valentin Chenka, "What is the problem here? To summon the watch commander requires the most serious of offenses. Now out with it! C'mon, man!"

Valentin Chenka's frail, thin frame stood in the doorway. His hands were numb from the evening's cold. His lanky legs were trembling. He began respectfully, "Your Honor, sir, he's come again. That one who calls himself 'Konstantin, the author.' Night after night he paces back and forth mumbling to himself. Then, at about one thirty in the morning, he drums up the nerve to climb the few steps to my flat and proceeds to knock softly on the door. If I don't answer, he starts wailing, 'Valentin! We had a contract. 100,000 rubles...the stories, the poems...' He goes on and on until I threaten to call you. Then, he leaves."

"Well, man," the watch commander, Semashkon began, "did you strike some deal with this gentleman?"

"Of course not," replied Valentin. He went on to explain, "You see, sir, I am Valentin Chenka, ex-clerk. I am forty, now a pianist. Well, I play at the cathedral on Sundays. During the week, I tally the census for the Minister of the People's Court, your lordship. And this Konstantin Bezuchken, I think it is...well, he's carrying this god-forsaken old satchel of some sort, crammed with torn papers and bound yellow pages. Lord knows how he makes heads or...anyway, he's always trying to prove to me that he's some writer as I said. He then starts to read the same lines over and over again, then brings this contract thing up and, well, you know the rest."

"What does he read to you?"

"Something about man's destiny. It goes something like this: The reality as you know it couldn't
even be set down as truth by God himself.
It is the unthinkable, the very aspects of life
which we deny that are, for all practical purposes—reality.
Go beyond that which is encompassed within the five senses, and while doing, remember fear is a sense.

8

If that which radiates as the sun,
if that which unfolds as a flower,
if these are from an origin, then
why not regress? Is it not the
source we seek? Why do we look
at the grains of sand separately?
Why not look at the entire beach?
For just as a volcano spews forth its

molten lava—we stand at the fringes of this "fear." To the center! This is where we will find all that is within. And all that is within is the source. So I say unto you, is reality, truth? Is truth, the reality? It's unthinkable!'"

Valentin's voice stopped, then he remarked to the watch commander, "He starts to cry, and he leaves."

"Do you know where he goes?" "No."

"Very well, we'll be on the lookout. I advise you to restrain yourself from answering your door—at all costs."

"Yes, sir. Good night!"

"Good morning, you mean!"

"Oh yes, of course, sir. I beg your pardon."

The sun came up over the city of St Petersburg, rising above the banks of the Neva, melting the early frost and causing the blades of grass in Akady Park to glisten under its rays. Beneath a birch tree, lay old Konstantin Bezuchken curled up like a fox. His withered hands were just able to brush off the frost and birch droppings that served as his blankets through the night.

Konstantin took his customary path from the top of the hill down to the kiosk where Lena was counting out her papers and boiling water for tea. Without acknowledgment, Konstantin dutifully secured a broom, swept the area around the kiosk, took an old rag, and wiped off the countertops. Then, he neatly placed all the newspapers in their respective racks. Lena smiled, "Spasibo, Konstantin, here's your tea and bread. Where are you off to today, my great author?"

His eyes wide open, a smile on his face, Konstantin proudly announced, "Today, I am scheduled to speak with the Minister of Arts and Culture. I am preparing a dissertation entitled, 'The Treasures of Cheops Tomb—The Ones You Didn't Know About.'" He rambled on, "You see, I have first-hand evidence that shows exactly where…"

And with this, Lena was interrupted by a customer. She greeted her customer and became engaged in a discussion about the latest government decrees. Konstantin simply turned, hung his head, and walked away in silence, heading for the government agency of Arts and Culture.

Once there, he proudly announced himself to the doorman, who in turn stared, perplexed for an instant. Then the doorman broke out in laughter and gasped, "You? You rag-tag old hunch-back. What could you offer the Minister of Arts and Culture? Are your rags antiques? I suppose relics from Peter the Great's closet!"

Two other guards began to laugh. Konstantin was grief stricken. He pleaded and begged, but it was to no avail. The guards grasped Konstantin by the arms and escorted him across the street. The doorman followed, ordering Konstantin, "Come back and I'll order the guards to shoot you!"

Konstantin shouted back, "Buy why? What have I done? Why would you shoot a famous author who has an appointment with…"

"Because," one of the guards began, "you've lost your buttons on your yak coat, you haven't bathed in years, and you're a crazy old fool." And with that the guard lowered and aimed his rifle in a mock gesture of threat at poor old Konstantin.

He departed. This time to the banks of the Neva, to Rashkosk Station. Once there, he sat on the bank, opened his satchel, and began to rummage through it as if looking for something very important.

Finally, he pulled out a crumpled paper. Squinting, he took the yellowed parchment in his trembling hands and began to read.

Valentin couldn't sleep. In one respect, he became irritated at the old pest that always showed up, but on the other hand, he really did feel sorry for him. He decided that he would make an attempt to seek information regarding this Konstantin Bezuchken After all, he was a census taker and had access to government files.

He dressed, drank a cup of tea, and summoned a cab. The driver inquired, "To where?"

Valentin replied, "Hurry, to the census bureau." The coachman whipped up his horses and they were off at a gallop. For seven days and late into each night, Valentin searched the records for a Konstantin Bezuchken. He had no success. He began to worry. Konstantin hadn't shown up in a week. There might be something wrong. Returning home on the eighth evening, at around 11:00 p.m., Valentin was surprised to find Watch Commander Semashkon and Police Commissioner Yuri Grezhkov. Neighbors were lurking about, curious as to why there were so many constables around, let alone the commissioner himself. Valentin tapped Victor on the shoulder, "Your lordship, is there a problem, sir?"

"Have you been home tonight?" Victor demanded.

"No, sir. I was at the county office, putting in some overtime. Why?"

"Because, that old Konstantin won't be badgering you anymore. Someone slit his throat on your porch."

"My God!" Valentin was visibly upset.

Just then, the commissioner summoned Victor and exclaimed, "It wasn't murder at all. There's blood all over his own hands. And they've just found a razor in the bushes. To top it all, here's a suicide note and an essay entitled, 'Destiny,' by Konchev Bezstanuch."

"Konchev Bezstanuch?" Valentin mumbled to himself. With that, Valentin raced on foot the entire twenty blocks back to the census bureau. There he searched again. And within ten minutes came upon a folder with the name, 'Konchev Bezstanuch.' Valentin opened the file. Inside he found records of the aforementioned person living at 210 Pladovodsky. Valentin was in shock! That was next door to him! But the fire burned that very same apartment down ten years ago before Valentin moved in.

He read further and discovered a woman's name on the document naming her as landlady; one Anastasia Kuznetzov, 209 Pladovodsky! The very same lady that Valentin bought the property from! She died in her sleep some five years earlier. Suddenly, he found a will by Anastasia made out to Valentin Azorzkij.

"My God!" Valentin thought out loud. "No wonder! The old man was right!" Valentin read on, 'The sum of 100,000 rubles shall be paid of one Konchev Bezstanuch for Valentin Azorzkij, who passed away last March, who had an agreement with this great twenty-year-old prospering author, Konchev, who was recently arrested by the Czar for mere trifles. Nevertheless, my Valentin had a contract with Konchev, and I want to honor this contract..."

"But why," wondered Valentin, "would this Konchev change his name?" Then it came to him. "Because he probably escaped, or when he was released, he dared not try to write, publish, or even lay claim to his own name."

Valentin walked slowly back to his flat. When he arrived, the streets were empty. The only sound was the hum of the new electric light pole that had recently been installed. Valentin approached the door. As he was about to open it, he found the old satchel and a note attached to it. It read: "Valentin, we've examined some of the contents of this bag and found it to be of no value to us. The suicide note left instructions for this to be left with 'Valentin.'" The suicide ended, "Valentin, if you can't make good on our contract, for God's sake please make good on publishing my work, for all mankind needs to learn my lessons! Signed, Konchev Bezstanuch.'"

Twenty years later, a now elderly Valentin Chenka arose, walked slowly to the podium, and began to address the crowded lecture hall at the University of Moscow's main library. "Dear Friends. We are here to honor a Russian hero. One who has in his death changed the living as it shall never be again. His short stories, his novels, his poetry—it has touched us all, brought us all together, and gave us wisdom, courage, and motivation.

"So in honor of the late Konchev Bezstanuch, true Russian patriot and author, I present this bank note to the Moscow State Library for the sum of 100,000 rubles. As for me, I swear I will continue to spread, worldwide, the great works of a master. The master of devotion to a country and the master of the teaching of compassion to his fellow man."

With that, Valentin felt a cold chill come upon him. Just then and there, he knew that an author's agony had finally come to an end.

Spring 1998

Success—Find It Anyplace

Many people are misled by the word success. They also confuse this word with other words: self-esteem, confidence, power, responsibility, and worst of all, MONEY!

* * *

A groom, all of five feet two, woke up early in the morning, went outside to his trailer, fed his horses, and began mucking stalls. Now, if you have never mucked a stall before you should be informed that it is a dirty, strenuous activity that requires total dedication to the cause itself.

Another man, six feet two, woke up, got dressed, kissed his wife good-bye, exited his three-story mansion, hopped into his Cadillac Seville, and drove the twenty-five miles into town to the county courthouse, where he was a lawyer. Now, if you have never been a lawyer, you should be informed that it takes much intelligence and dedication to the cause itself.

To refer back to the groom cleaning stalls; he was clad in blue jeans, boots, and a baseball cap. Methodically in the course of the three hours he put all the solid straw and manure into a large pile in the middle of the stall. Next he pushed the still, unused straw aside, up against the wall. He then put all the dirty straw into the muck cart, and then spread the unused straw back over the entire surface. Next, he went to the feed room and carried back on his pitchfork fine flakes of new straw. He put it in the middle and carefully spread the new bedding out in layers, all the while banking the sides higher (so the center would contain all the moisture). Each stall took him twenty to thirty minutes, until all ten were finished and he was exhausted, yet very self-pleased and very content. He was proud. He was— "successful."

The lawyer spent the next six hours haggling with a judge, convincing a jury and outsmarting the prosecution. With intrigue, intuition, and a command of the law, he presented his case masterfully and was able to get his client acquitted of all charges!

"Not guilty!" the jury exclaimed. He felt belated, self-confident, and proud. He was— "successful."

The lawyer drove back home, greeted his wife, took off his suede jacket and leather shoes, and sat down in his recliner and sipped a fine glass of wine.

The groom went into his trailer, took off his boots and his base-ball cap, and sat down in his aluminum-folding chair and sipped a glass of cheap beer.

The lawyer thought, It was a successful day. The groom thought, It was a successful day.

Yes, both men were proud. This word PRIDE, not the others, represents "success."

Three Wise Indians

Once upon a time in the beautiful brown mountains of North Carolina, a state located on the East Coast of the United States, there were three Indian tribes. The three tribes were the Shoshone, Cherokee, and the Choctaw.

Each tribe lived on three separate mountains. The Shoshone lived on the mountain that was the highest, the Cherokee lived on the medium-sized mountain and the Choctaw lived on the smallest mountain.

The Shoshone Indians had all the trees to build huts to live in. The Cherokee Indians had a big lake and had all the water to drink. And the Choctaw had all the deer for food.

This created a great problem. You see, one tribe started to fight with the other two tribes, trying to take control of what they had. Then, the other two tribes started to fight the others, trying to do the same thing.

So, you ended up with the Cherokee, the Shoshone, and the Choctaw all fighting each other for the three things that they all needed to survive: food, water, and shelter.

One day, a young Cherokee boy went to get a bucket of water at the lake. At the same time, he saw a Shoshone boy carrying wood and a Choctaw carrying deer meat.

The three boys were scared at first, but being young and curious they went up to each other and began to talk.

"Hi!" the Cherokee boy began. "My name is Running Elk."

"Hi!" the Choctaw boy said. "My name is Grey Wolf."

"Hi!" the Shoshone boy replied. "My name is Little Eagle."

The boys began to talk about the wars that had been fought for years over the trees, the water, and the deer meat. They started to argue that each of their own tribe had the right to own everything. The boys argued until all three picked up stones and began to threaten each other.

Suddenly, dark, gray clouds appeared in the sky. The three boys stopped arguing. Running Elk said, "It's going to rain and we won't make it back."

Grey Wolf replied, "I'm scared that my family will miss me." Little Eagle advised, "We need to build a shelter." He offered, "I will give my wood to build the hut."

Grey Wolf offered, "I will give you my deer meat so we may eat."

Running Elk offered, "I will give you my water so we may drink."

All the boys worked together and built a wooden hut. It began to rain very hard. It rained for two weeks and the boys had to stay in the hut. They shared the deer meat and the water.

Meanwhile, the three tribes had sent out search parties to look for the boys. The search parties just happened to find the boys at the same time. The Indians were about to fight again, but Running Elk, Grey Wolf, and Little Eagle all came out of the hut holding hands.

That night, the Cherokee, Shoshone, and Choctaw chiefs met and they praised the boys for their brave actions. They decided that they would share the wood, the water, and the food from now on.

To this day, all three tribes live together in peace.

Riders Up!

"As they turn for home, it's Onward Go by a nose. Driving hard on the rail is Lemon Drop, followed by Who's Who in the middle of the racetrack…"

"Under no circumstances should you use your whip. You are to sit tight until the eighth pole, then throw another cross and hand ride him the rest of the way home."

Those were trainer Vera MacNamera's only instructions prior to the race.

"Who's Who is now charging hard, closing ground in the middle of the racetrack, but Onward Go still has the lead by a length. Lemon Drop has fallen back to third. My Upset is now gaining ground…"

With each stride, I threw another cross, took a shorter hold and pumped my hands forward on Onward's neck. My back was level, my feet straight back, and my knees pressed against the withers. I felt as if I was stretched out, flying on a magic carpet.

Suddenly, Onward Go responded to the newest hold with unprecedented speed. He opened up by a length, then two, and finally three.

Yet, the ever-present thunderous pounding of the other horses hitting the turf coupled with their rhythmic breathing, reminded me that they were not far behind, and that the race was not finished.

At the eighth pole, I was tempted to cock my whip and use it on Onward's massive torso. However, Vera's explicate orders resounded in my ears:

"DON'T GO TO THE STICK!"

I concentrated as hard as I could, affixing my eyes to the finish line in front of me. Pushing and driving with all of my remaining strength, I hoped that Onward Go could hang on.

However, I had nothing to fear. His enormous, seventeen-hand body collected himself for a final time. His stride became that of a gazelle, and his heart, the heart of a champion, surfaced.

"...Down the stretch it's Onward Go by three lengths, as Who's Who is fading rapidly. My Upset is third by a nose. And Onward Go is the winner by three and one-half lengths..."

* * *

"Paul, I need more light on this side of his face. Good, hold it there...that's it...got it! Corey, I have two more left."

"Ken, what do you think?"

"Well, he needs to get his butt down, his hands down—you know, little things like that."

"Mike, reach out more, take a shorter hold, and angle your whip up about 10 degrees. That's perfect. Great! Oh man, you look good now!"

Finally! January 17, 1975. Portland Meadows. After a year of twelve-hour days—mucking stalls, walking hots, grooming and galloping horses—after giving up my family, my education, my... myself, I had accomplished what I had been praying for from the beginning; I had won my first horse race.

"And the seventh race is official, ladies and gentlemen. Onward Go is the winner, Who's Who is second, and My Upset is third. Your attention please. This was apprentice jockey Mike Dixon's first career win."

Now what! More grapefruit, tuna salads, diet pills, and insomnia! What color will my bruises be tomorrow, blue or black! Will I pass out from being weak, and will that big chestnut colt run off with me again, because I just COULDN'T hold him anymore?

What happened to taking infield and batting practice all day and then munching out at Pizza Hut all night? "One year," they say. Just one year and I'll be leading bug boy. Damn those baseball scouts that took me off the field and brought me to the racetrack! Them and their three Big "D's": Determination, Dedication, Discipline. Damn them to hell!

* * *

"Paul, again, more light on the left side. Mike, hold your arm, don't move it. Hold absolutely still! Good. Okay, let's shoot!" For a one-horse field, that was the toughest horse race I had ever ridden. Not because it was six furlongs, or two miles, but because it lasted for two hours! It took all the endurance I could muster to make it to the finish line in one piece. My knees swelled up to the size of watermelons, my back felt like it had a knife plunged in it, and both my calves had been mercilessly stretched beyond their elasticity.

"Ken, should I have a half or a full cross? What part of the race are we doing now? Christ, the withers on this mare are killing me. Can't we change mounts?"

No, we couldn't. It was the only oil drum for miles around.

A two-month long racing career, coupled with four years of galloping horses, hadn't been for nothing. Even after doing a stint in the navy and returning to school to get my BA in Russian, I couldn't be "set down."

Thus, following eight hours of posing as a model, I was hand-ed a check for $600. I had earned more money and more fame PRETENDING to be a jockey than I had done when I really was a jockey!

"Thanks for your help, Mike." "No problem, Corey. Anytime."

The advertising executive gleamed as he surveyed the final prints that were to be used to advertise the 1984 Del Mar Thoroughbred Racing Season.

* * *

What is that old saying: "Stranger things have happened"?

Who knows; I may wake up tomorrow only to find that I have grown a foot, put on twenty pounds, and have been selected National League Player of the Week.

Well, okay! Not that strange. "Riders Up!"

Happy New Year, Boris Simyonovich

1888, Rekov, a small village on the outskirts of Moscow.

"Hey Simyonovich! You old clout head! What are you doing to bring in the New Year?"

"Huh, he's probably sitting at home with his cat and that old blind dog. Or are you going to dance in the streets again for us, you crazy buzzard? Ah! Ah! Ah!"

"Yes, you durachok! Party it up! All three of you loony toons. Sit at home like a band of stoolies, eating stale black bread, sipping rotten cider, and listening to that archaic classical music from France."

The three men sitting on the rickety straw chairs in the corner of Pavlov's Bar were quite a sight. All three amused themselves with card games and tales as they smoked their rolled cigarettes and drank cheap vodka.

Stephan, the youngest and first to speak, was a banker. He had a fat belly and pocked-marked swollen cheeks. His head was as shiny as a piece of china, and he sat there stooped over in a drunken stupor, jesting and poking fun at poor old Boris.

Ivanov was a tall, frail old geezer of sixty. He hated animals and liked to tease small children. Ivanov used to beat Boris' dog with a stick while passing in front of the premises on the way to Pavlov's.

Then, there was Isaac, fifty-seven, well built, broad-shouldered, with deep-set black eyes and meaner than a Russian black bear. He had had twenty children by seven wives and was pursuing his eighth, though some say he had even a ninth in mind! Isaac hated anything nice and did what he could to put the Simyonovich household down whenever possible.

Boris Simyonovich was a kind, gentle, elderly gent of seventy-five. Of small stature, he had sea blue eyes, small weathered hands, and a delicate, sympathetic smile.

They say old Simyonovich was crazy. It was said that he would sit up all through the night, singing to his cat Sasha and dog Kulak, while all the time playing on a wooden flute, which was given to him by his great-grandfather when he was all but four.

Simyonovich lived in a one-room, log cabin that was located in the middle of a pine forest. There was a small creek nearby where Sasha would lead old Kulak down to the water's edge, while Boris himself sat passively, somberly on the bank, and reminisced about what was, and was now, all but gone—a wife, a baby daughter, and a beautiful home in the village.

Yes, there were many strange oddities about Boris Simyonovich. The one that stood out in everyone's mind was the time that the jealous Afanasov Oglander slipped a potion into Boris' cider on New Year's Eve some twenty years ago. Simyonovich, as the story goes, went absolutely mad, setting afire his hay sticks, praying to a piece of bark on a tree he mistook for an icon, and feeding his chickens poisoned mushrooms. To top matters off, he ran naked down Mayovsky Street, playing his flute and singing "Volare" at the top of his lungs.

Oh, but this charade wasn't over yet. Our dear, poor Boris performed the most despicable of all acts. Innocently, he sided up to all the single women in two taverns, kissing each squarely as if they were his own. When the count was over, Simyonovich had kissed a total of one hundred and twenty-eight maidens, proposed to twenty, and had five accepted!

January 1, 1889, found Boris Simyonovich passed out atop an old oak tree in front of the mayor's house, where I might add he had dashed in, stole a kiss from the lordship's three daughters, his wife, and the lordship himself!

He awoke in a puzzled daze. He knew not where he was or where he had been. But, he quickly became familiar with the shackles that were around his hands and feet, and the policemen who had drug him off to jail.

He lay in the corner all crumpled up. He looked like a filthy scoundrel mutt that had been kicked and beaten. Bruised from climbing in the tree, his head mercilessly on fire, he remained in jail for two days. On the third day, they led Boris into the courtroom and passed a quick and painful sentence: one month in jail, a 500-ruble fine, and, to add insult to the jury, banishment from the village.

Shortly thereafter, Boris' wife, Elena, divorced him and married that very scum, Afanasov, who himself turned the dirty trick against poor Simyonovich. Some say it was a jealous plot; others say it was just a hoax. Nevertheless, Simyonovich lost everything and was demoted to a class much lower than that of a peasant, but slightly higher than a beggar.

Boris arose, gave a slight glance at the three old drunks, and exited Pavlov's. He made his way down the cobblestone street that led away from the tavern to the edge of the forest. On his way, he passed many pubs, eating establishments, and households, where much merry-making was taking place in anticipation of the New Year.

Boris suffered much during the course of a year, but not as much as at New Year. He would go home tonight, as he had in the past, sitting sadly in his old rocker, his cat, and dog at his feet, eating his stale bread, and sipping the bad cider. Then, with memories of warmth and remorse, he'd sit until dawn, playing the same French melody that played that very night, some twenty years ago. Boris Simyonovich would mumble unintelligibly and dreary thoughts out loud until finally, the lonely New Year would force him to sleep.

But the laughing and the jesting had gotten to him too much tonight. He was in a particularly bad state. As he was about to enter the edge of the forest he came upon a half-clothed, tear-faced little girl of about five, clutching her one-eyed dolly and whimpering, "Mommy, Mommy. Why did you leave me? Why?"

Boris Simyonovich was stunned. He stooped over, looked into the poor child's eyes, and asked, "What happened to my little one?" Sobbing uncontrollably, she gazed up at the poor man with a twinkle in her eye and began to ramble and stuttering from fright, "I, I…sir… liv… live on south Yaraslovsky Street, building six, house number for…forrr…ty-ni…nine. I, I was riding in the…the cart with… with Mommy, sit…sitting behind the sacks of flour. She hit a bump and I came tum-b-ling out. I, I'm lost now."

Searching for the right thing to say, Simyonovich looked into a pair of very familiar eyes and compassionately comforted our little orphan, "Do not fear, little angel. I'll take you home myself."

"You will?" the little girl asked with astonishment.

"Sure," said Simyonovich, and off the pair went, hand in hand, back down the cobblestone street that led to Prosepesky Boulevard, which led to Yaraslovsky Street, building number six, house number forty-nine.

"Well, we're here, mister. But, I don't think a soul's in sight. They must be searching for me. Could you come in and wait for mommy and tell her the whole story?"

"Sure child. Sure. But, you have yet to tell me your name."

And wearing a shrewd smirk, she replied, "My name is Alexandra Borisovich…"

With this, the little girl swung open the huge wooden engraved door. Taking Boris by the hand, she led him into a large, white stucco mansion with lavender curtains and wooden paneling on the walls. It was very dark inside and Alexandra turned to Boris and blurted with warmth, "Welcome home, Grandfather."

Just then, candle lights appeared from every room, singing began, and the images of three old men could be seen dancing off the walls. They were Stephan, Ivanov, and Isaac, each holding bottles of wine and dishes of hors d'oeuvres.

Suddenly, Isaac shrieked out, "There will be no stale bread and rotten cider for you this New Year's, my friend!" With that, he offered Boris caviar and champagne. Ivanov wound up the phonograph and "Volare" began to play. Stephan picked up Boris' wooden flute and handed it to him saying, "Sing, old man. Fill your heart with joy."

Then, from nowhere, an eloquent silver-haired lady descend-ed the stairs. She was accompanied by a younger, attractive, twenty-year-old maiden.

Alexandra triumphantly shouted, "Now Granddaddy, do you believe me? My name is Alexandra Borisovich Simyonovich!" Boris Simyonovich could not speak. He was dumbfounded. He gazed at his wife, his daughter, and his granddaughter, collapsed on the divan, put his hands in his lap, and began to weep. Tears of joy flowed down his wrinkled face like waterfalls.

As if this wasn't enough, the mayor of Rekov himself appeared and exclaimed to all, "Let it be known that our dear, old friend, Simyonovich, is here to stay."

Isaac, Stephan, and Ivanov each hugged Boris. Ivanov declared, "No more feuding, friend. We've turned a bad deed. We're sorry. Forgive us, brother. We know the truth now, and that scoundrel Afanasov will pay dearly. God bless you, Boris Simyonovich."

Elena sat by Boris' side on the divan. Simyonovich raised his flute to his lips and began to play along with "Volare." Kulak lay down, Sasha purred softly, and Alexandra fell asleep in her grandfather's lap.

Happy New Year, Boris Simyonovich.

A very lonely time for me. Life is not fair. Yet I've not been fair to life. It will be a Good year, though, God trust.

Hurray, Boris!

Happy Ever After

"Hey, Nikolaj! What the hell is wrong with you? You look as if you've seen death a thousand times. What's wrong? Can't find an ending to a story? Or has the ocean's waves swallowed your soul up? My God, Nikolaj Nikolaiovich, this sorrow! It can't be that bad this time...Or can it be? Come, lad. Let's go to Blar-ney's, have a bass, mimic some lyrics, and make requests...Come, Nikolaj, let's go..."

"No, Isaac. You go. You have fun. My heart is heavy and it seems as if the time it will take to lessen the burden will alone kill me. Take today, for instance. It all started off so genuine, so meaningful...

"We met at 8:30 a.m., walked the three blocks to the lake, all the while talking, laughing, and sharing anecdotes and interests. We walked and jogged, teased each other, and made funny faces and comments about snakes and fat people.

"Her short, blonde hair, bubbly smile, and glistening eyes— ev-ery time she'd look my way, I glanced downward, hoping that she wouldn't read my eyes, guess my thoughts, or ask me an embarrassing question.

"We talked of cycling, gourmet food, wine, and love affairs. She told me how she would soon sell her jewelry to some affluent merchant and steal away to the Riviera.

"Then, I told her of Baham, my sacred Iranian friend, who died while seeking 'Jahad' through Allah. I told her how special it was to talk about him, and I know she knew, because tears welled in her eyes and she caught me staring up at the ceiling. It was obvious she understood. She fell silent.

"Soon, 9:30 turned into 11:45. I looked into her eyes for a final time and saw a similarity between both of us, a sincerity, a need to be loved and a strong desire to give love and the willingness to turn all bad into good. I hugged her inside, walked her to her apartment, and left as solemnly and as quickly as I had arrived.

"We met again at three. She shared her art with me, her success, and asked me if I knew where she might sell her wares. I just marveled at her talent and was so impressed with her positive attitude that I forgot to answer her. When I did, she was off on another sentence, 'Frank is very supportive of my work; that's one thing I can say for him.'

"Shortly after this, we went to eat dinner- Mexican food. We drank beer- she Carta Blanca, IN Bohemia. We laughed, teased each other again, and sought each other's advice. We talked for two hours (about a few things I dare not mention, for my reader would lose all respect for me!) Then it was time to meet her friend at his work, an insurance company, where we ended up some fifteen minutes later.

"Then it happened. Her friend mentioned this coming weekend, a man named Jack and what he looked like. She even went to Jack's desk and wrote him a bizarre note. Next, and this is where it must have hit me, they went on and on about going here and there, with him, and so on and so on.

"I went to the patio area and sometime later she checked up on me and asked what I was doing. 'Looking around,' I replied.

"At this point, I suddenly realized that either she, or I, was a fool and had been for quite some time.

"I drove her and her friend to the mall. I went to the bookstore, they went to jewelry shops. At 8:45 we left for home. Once there, thank yous and good-byes were exchanged.

"Fifteen minutes later she called and inquired about a ride to La Jolla. My God, Isaac! Did she really think I'd have refused? I mean, I would have given anything to have been with her, if only for her gaiety, warmth, and sincerity.

"Then, I sat down and wrote a story about how people interact, what they want out of life, and how one makes their dreams come true. It wasn't easy, but I finally came to the conclusion in the story that we all want that special person, a special relationship. We don't know how to go about finding it. And, if and when we do, we either throw it away like fools or pass by it like a blind man.

"So, Isaac, go...Go to Blarney's, have a bass, and make a special request for me. Me, I'll go home and figure out an ending to that story you mentioned about. It's about a man and a woman, how they met, fell in love, married, and lived—HAPPILY EVER AFTER!

"Good night, Isaac. Go with God."

"God be with you, Nikolaj Nikolaiovich."

Shavings or Straw?
(The Feed Store)

"No! That's not a trash truck! A trash truck is an enormous metal box with a piston inside that compacts the garbage. This is anything but! Why, how nonsensical! It's not even rubbish. Why, we're talking…uh! …Well, it is a big metal box about 20x8x8. It has an opening at one end. The opening has two giant doors that are secured with a sliding rod and a hasp…no…well, anyway this metal box sits on this flatbed truck you see…don't interrupt me, please! I am trying to explain something to you! Okay, now, as I was saying, this big truck (mainly because it has a big engine), hauls it around…what does it haul in the big metal box? Well, I'll tell you what it hauls. IT HAULS SHAVINGS! SOFT AND FLUFFY WOODEN SHAVINGS!

"So this truckload of shavings comes three times a week. There's 'CROWN' and there's 'LONG BEACH' shavings. But there is a huge difference between them! You see, THE MOST distinguishing, important characteristic is that CROWN shavings come in plastic bags, are only forty pounds (or seven cubic feet of loose sawdust), and have bugs in them. Whereas the LONG BEACH shavings come machine-wrapped and are packed tightly in a strong, one-inch thick paper (just like the old paper grocery bags), are fifty pounds, and have no bugs...the bugs? Yeah, little black critters! They bite the heck out of your arms when you're movin' them bags, man. Itch like heck that night too. Can hardly get a wink of sleep...

"Okay...well, the driver he's usually a tall fellow so he can reach the top of the metal box. Then, he backs the truck up, raises the bed, and dumps. Well, it really slides off on its own, down a little rail, then it gets dropped off on the ground, hard! Sounds like a clap-a-thunder it does...Yeah, gets put between the hot-walker and the feed barn, that's where ya pick'em up...huh? No, man! We load em. Then, the guys from the feed store, Tony and Denny, both come by in their flatbed truck. It's smaller than the shaving's truck, but a flatbed is just the same. They back up in front of the bin as close as possible and start loading. Tony usually climbs up and throws the bags down to Denny for him to stack. They're easy to stack too 'cause they come square and packet tight, except the CROWN... What? Yeah, we deliver too; $10 charge for every half ton...

"It's possible to load seventy bags onto the flatbed. First, you place two bags lengthwise from left to right, in the left-hand corner, as far forward as possible. You place a third alongside...uh, pardon me? Yes! We have flax seed too! As I was sayin', alongside those two, as in north to south, as opposed to east to west. Now and then there are two more side by side W-E as opposed to N-S placed next. You now have five bags down. You repeat the process again, only this time you reverse the direction of the first two bags and the last two bags in order that they are in an interlocking position. You usually stack four rows high and three rows back. Pardon? Yes, a pickup is fine. What kind? Ford? F50? Yes, it'll work.

"Now, upon completion of the stacking, you get into the truck and PROCEED very, VERY SLOWLY (so as not to upset any of the bags) to the barns, which require that they be restacked because in those barns there are stalls, that sleep the finest racehorses in the country, here at the fabulous San Luis Rey Downs Thoroughbred Training Center, right here in Bonsall, California. And, I might add, these very same horses prefer to sleep on shavings instead of plain old straw.

"Uh?... oh yes, the horses like the shavings, lady. They tell me it's really soft...uh? Yeah, I've always been able to talk to horses... oh really? You don't say? Talk to goats do you?

"Well, three other reasons too. You see, those stems from the straw leave markings on the horses' skin after sleepin' and the grooms don't like that. Hard to rub out I guess. And the stems poke the horses in the eyes and it irritates 'em. The last reason is the most important I guess. You see, the straw don't soak up the pee, but the shavings do...price ma'am? Well, straw is $2.50 a bail, whereas shavings are $5.00 for the LONG BEACH, because of the grocery store paper being more expensive. Now, the CROWN, they are $4.50 only, 'cause they come in 'packed' plastic bags...

"Use? Yes, ma'am, grooms say, 'Easier to work with. Use a shovel instead of a pitchfork anytime.'

"Trainer says, 'Little more money, but better for the horses. Besides, owners pay anyway.'

"But the horse says, 'Whinny, whinny, whinny! Can't live without 'em—that's horse talk ma'am.

"See ma'am, you have to look at the entire matter in general: stacking bags of shavings, delivering them, changing them every day. You see, it does require a keen eye, physical strength, and a...pardon? Yes. We're open from 9-3, Mon-Sat. Just tell the guard at the main gate that you're going to the feed store. That's the San Luis Rey Downs Feed Store, 561-0307, but remember, we ARE closed on Sundays...thank-ya see ya soon ma'am...thanks again... no, no trouble ma'am...bye now.

"Wow! Some people are so hard to convince!"

* * *

The guard's voice came over the loudspeaker, "Feed store, customer. Tony, Denny, or Mike, go to the feed store. A lady wants to buy shavings."

First Day on Welfare

It was 9:30 a.m. Where were all the people? I thought there was a 7 percent unemployment rate. The "Employment Services" department was almost empty when I walked through the double glass doors that led either straight ahead to the information line or to the left, the interview line. Across from these two lines on the other side of the room, there was a large black-and-white sign hanging from the ceiling that read: "JOB SEARCH LINE FORMS HERE."

As I approached the information line, I saw a middle-aged woman clad in stained blue slacks and an old wrinkled white blouse. She was leaning over the counter and listening passively to the official's instructions, "Go home. Wait three more days. Mail the form, then wait again. It's simple; you need only to follow the directions and not be so impatient. Now, next please…"

The lady's face was a figment of fatigue, despair, desolation, hard nights, long days, and hangovers. I felt sad for her, but also somewhat unsympathetic. After all, she chose her life. The lady must now suffer the consequences.

She glanced over at me, then left the building. "Sir! May I help you? Sir!"

I proceeded to the counter. As I did I felt very tense, humiliated, and ashamed. Looking up, I found a pair of beautiful, hazel-blue eyes staring at me belonging to a beautiful woman. Blonde hair fell at her side, so radiant, so intriguing.

I wanted to blurt out that I was an instructor's aide, a graduate student of Russian, and a current this and a former that. Furthermore, I needed only one month's relief until my new, guaranteed job commenced in the fall.

Instead, I froze. All thoughts escaped me. This beautiful woman now became the very goddess of my destiny. "Hmm," she began, reading the form that had been sent to me a week earlier from the district office. She continued in a very business-like tone, "You, sir, have a job in September?"

"Yes, ma'am," I replied politely, with a hint of deliverance in my voice.

"Says here your work ended on June 16. No work since then?"

"Well, ma'am, I was a bus monitor for two hours a day, at $6 an hour. I volunteered the rest of my time until noon. From noon until supper, I worked elsewhere."

As if to entrap me she shot back, "Doing what?" "Writing a novel," I replied matter-of-factly. "That's not work!" she snapped.

"Ah, ma'am! This is work! This, ma'am! Lest we forget the endless hours of work and effort by Poe, Tolstoy, and Twain? And the copies they sold?"

"I'm sorry, sir, but dealing with your dreams and personal fantasies are not in my job description!"

I declared vehemently, "Nor is castigating or humiliating someone!"

She handed me a handful of forms, the last of which was a 3x5 card. She scribbled, "8-6-85, 2 pm. Group P." With that, I bid my fair lady a good day, gathered the needed documents, nodded, then exited the building and onto the streets of El Cajon. The sun was shining bright. Its heat could be felt by the wilt-ing leaves on the plum trees. Heat could be seen on the streets the way the water rose on the black asphalt street and quenched your thirst.

I decided to go to the library, a ten-minute walk down Magnolia to the center of town. Once there, I worked on a translation of a Soviet short story, then filled out the documents that I had been given, and finally read two more chapters in "Quiet Flows the Don."

When I returned to the employment department, it was about 1:45 p.m. There were already many people sitting in the chairs that aligned the wall on the east side of the building. Again, I walked up to the counter where my eyes met yet another sign stating: "Group interview at 2pm. Be Seated."

I felt annoyed, separated, and cheated by the bureaucracy; I was aghast! "For $30 a week? For a month? BS! I paid into this; my employer paid into this. What is so difficult about THE procedure?"

Then I realized why. I scanned the seats, stared at the people, and immediately figured out why. They all felt like me! Panicked, disoriented, grieved, and indignant at their government, their home! It was easy now. It was pitiful and sad.

At 2:15, a short, bald middle-aged man entered through a side door, waved to all of us, and then made the most degrading comment to us. "All those who are here to collect wel..., uh, employment insurance benefits, please come with me."

We were led into a room with two large tables and on top were packets in front of each seat. We seated ourselves and waited for instructions.

"Excuse me, lady," the bald-headed fellow began, "uh, no children allowed." Until now, these very kids had been doodling in their coloring books, making games out of visiting the drinking fountain, and going to the restroom to play with the electric hand dryers. Their mother had to remind them on many occasions, "Sit down, Johnny. Be quiet, now. ..."

Our bald 'friend's' name was Terry Rolland. "Call me T. R. man. Don't ask why; it's a long story and we need to get down to business."

I began to blurt loudly, "Hey, T. R...." "Yes, sir."

"Never mind, sir."

What I was going to ask him was if we were getting paid today.

"Does everyone have a pencil? Good. Now about your paper-work?"

A nod from us, a gesture from him. Now where's my check?

Next we were instructed to complete all the forms in the packets in front of us. A big robust lady sitting in front of me with a mop of red hair, wearing yellow pants, a green blouse, and a fake pearl necklace turned around and asked, "Does he mean these forms?"

Hi! I'm clueless... "Uh, no ma'am. He means the forms that are located on the third floor, room 2A. You don't have them?"

She actually got up, said, "Thank you, sir," and left.

She never came back. Well, considering the building had only one floor, I understand why...

"We're now going to see a brief film showing you how to fill out the remaining forms, look for jobs, make and receive weekly claims, and finally how to reapply to the program if you become unemployed again. Any questions?"

Here it comes. A big dude in the back...

"Yeah, man. What if you've always been unemployed?" Oh, well...

My mind started to drift. I began to think about the billions of dollars going out weekly to people who can work but won't. People who don't receive benefits and yet can't work. Something wasn't right. What's more, when the third and fourth generation is relying on this system for their inheritance, well then...

"Okay ladies and gentlemen, please pass in your forms. Next, I'll turn the program over to..."

The other door swung open and entered what I believe was the only way out of constant unemployment—the most beautiful woman in the world! I mean if a man had this, who would want to work?

Mary Lou, a country girl from Arkansas, was awesome. Her instructions were the only ones I followed all day, "Now you must look at least four times a week for a job. Then return the check-off sheet to my office. We'll review it, verify the information, and then the following week you can pick up your check, or we can mail it to you. Remember, you'll always be one week behind. Now, let's take the first form and go over it. Form 1A36592 'dash' 8, ..."

After an hour and a half of some nonsensical lecture, I realized that beauty is only skirt deep, literally, and that all I these forms, interviews, job searches, verifications, T. R. and the Arkansas woman, are what's costing the government and causing the deficit, not the insurance benefits!

I sat through it for the next fourteen days and followed the instructions to a tee. I brought back my forms weekly, etc., then one month later, the first day of my job, September 4, 1992, I received back a check for a grand total of $30.65!

Thus, ending the "First Day on Welfare."

Something Meant
for Someone Else

When I arrived at the banquet hall, I was out of breath and perspiring heavily. My nose was running from the frigid air, and it was difficult to see clearly through the thin layer of water that covered my burning eyes.

"Damn! I won't be introduced. They'll simply overlook me completely. Why? A dignitary such as me being late for his award. Absurd! Rude!"

I slipped silently through the massive oak doors that were left slightly ajar to allow the fresh air to seep into the immense building. As I did, I noticed everyone was eating expensive black Russian caviar and sipping Pinot Grigio champagne from fine Italian Dolani crystal. They were having a grand time, sitting about, dressed in their fine New York apparel, solving the contemporary problems of the world, and treating themselves as if they were the last human beings left on the face of the earth. It seemed so courtly, yet so despicable and false.

For some strange reason I thought that the entire assembly would notice that their long-awaited guest of honor had finally arrived, and that some grateful colleague would leap to his feet and announce proudly, "Ladies and Gentlemen! Distinguished guests! He's here! Look! The famous founder and editor of our much-coveted newspaper, THE SAN LUIS REY WIRE! Let us welcome our newest hero and friend!"

There were no such words of praise, friendly greetings, or hero's welcome of any kind, only solitude and indifference. At that point, I decided to divulge my long-awaited presence. I set out down the middle of the aisle and, having carefully calculated my paces with those of the oncoming waiter, intentionally collided with both him and the serving cart he was pushing. I thought I did it! Now they'll realize that I'm here and they'll take note of me. They will surely now stand and applaud me.

The entire hall burst out in laughter! However, I felt confident that this was their way to hide their embarrassment. Then, silence befell the room.

Stares of agonizing humiliation poured down upon me until I was on the verge of a social breakdown. Suddenly, from the very back of the dining hall a voice rang out, breaking the deafening silence, "IMBECILE!" This was followed by still another formal greeting, "CLUMSY OX!" Still, others, until the whole audience held nothing back, "IDIOT!" "MORON!"

When the heckling subsided and the stares wore off, a man who had been seated at the head of a long table at the front of the great hall arose and walked toward the podium. Straightening his lumping frame, the tall, slender, bearded gentleman began to address the crowd, "My dearest friends. My devoted citizens..."

Ah, and not a moment too late. At last. He will no doubt apologize for my infraction and proceed to introduce me to my loyal patrons.

Looking up at the audience, he continued, "May I have the pleasure and honor to introduce to you a man whom we have all come to grow quite fond of. A leader, a self-taught writer, who, realizing that our community was in such great despair, took it upon himself to create something that has brought the entire San Luis Rey River Valley together as one big family. A newspaper. A few simple pages are put together, with anecdotes, short stories, poems, and profiles about our very own people.

"We can never repay him for his sacrifices and for bringing this valley together, for instilling the much-needed pride and compassion in all of us, and for providing the motivation necessary to finally solve the many problems that beset us. Ladies and Gentlemen, may I..."

Stand up straight. Don't be shy. This is your moment. Whatever you do, don't trip over any chairs on the way up to the podium.

"I bring to you our very own Mr. Frank Baily!"

My heart fell to the bottom of my stomach. My knees buckled out from underneath me, and I fell hard to the floor face downward, and began to sob uncontrollably. It must have been a sight to see, for I remember slamming my forehead several times on the hard wooden surface until I became violently nauseous. I cried out in vain for people to help me. I began a speech of my own, one of pleading, one of acceptance. "No, I beg you! Those are my words on that paper. He's a fraud! He must not...thank you, kind people. Thank you for giving credit where credit is due. I forgive, and I am grateful..."

Just then, someone grabbed my arm and forced me to stand up. The tall gentleman removed his glasses and demanded of me, "What is your name? How dare you barge in here and make a mockery of this function and slander this fine gentleman."

"I, I am the true author of THE WIRE, Thomas Halley III, I started the paper at the racetrack across the valley. Surely you remember the date, December 3, 1978? Or how about the interviews with Mr. Frances, the great trainer, and with Mr. Wicker, the great owner? Why, I received a letter of invitation to be the guest of honor here tonight at 7:30, only my car broke down a few miles down the road and I had to run here. Please forgive me..."

Five huge figures moved toward me, while the room was filled with hysterical laughter and utter bewilderment. A state of mass confusion broke out all at once and conversations about the incident at hand were heard being struck up at every table. "Listen, you lunatic. For starters it is January 3, 1991! I don't know what it is you're trying to prove here, but it is time for you to exit the premises. NOW!"

With that, the five beastly men literally dragged me to the front door, opened it, and threw me back out into the arctic night air. As I lay on the dirt, my face caked with my own dried blood and my once-immaculate dark blue suit disheveled and torn to shreds, I could hear them all laughing and telling jokes about what had just taken place. Suddenly it dawned on me; I must get back to the tack room at once and ready this parody for tomorrow's issue.

* * *

All sixteen thoroughbreds stood patiently at the entrances to their stalls as I read my editorial aloud to them. Once in a while one would shake his head up and down in approval and still another would bite on his stall door in frustration, trying to persuade me to change a line here and there.

"Tommy! You still up? It's me, the security guard. Hey, listen, I just got word that there's a big disturbance going on over at the county club. It might make news for the paper."

"Thanks, Mac. I'll get on it right away."

After All, I Am You

So, Sergei, why do you do these things for people when in the end they scorn you? Where are you going today? To clean a stall for some trainer? To mop a floor for a restaurant owner? Maybe you are going to try to 'save' another soul down at that one-room schoolhouse you toil in day in and day out. Well, is that it Sergei? Oh, I know. You're not only going to plant Isaac's corn for him, you're going to buy the seed too—all for a pat on the back. No, now let's see…you mean you're going to Lady Sonya's house to tidy her room? To clean her kitchen?

Why, Sergei, do you even know yourself, what you're doing and why you're doing it?

My poor lad, haven't the crows picked at your sockets long enough? Have not the ravens tormented you a hundred fold? And what of Sasha? Cleared his field for a few melons in return, rotten ones at that. You fool, Sergei! You believe too much! You are TOO loyal! You endure too much! Sasha pleaded for you to stay. What happened? You stayed and cracked eggshells and got beaten for it!

Sergei, you imbecile! And now look at you. You're writing senseless words again that nobody will ever read. You're an old man now, Sergei. Better to let those who can provide do the providing.

Your brother Ivanov was right. Who would want to be with a hot-walker, a farmer, a fantasy writer, a potato planter, and a beekeeper? Nobody wants a jack-of-all-trades Sergei. Remember Ivanov telling you that "you are not meant to be anyone to someone"? You, as he said, are "just someone for anyone!"

It's time, Sergei, to stop dreaming of a life that will never be. So where ARE you going, my man? To sweep Afanovsov's store? Maybe he'll give you some candies heh? Or, better go brush Alexander's horses. God knows the groom is a lazy drunkard who gets paid for doing almost nothing, and we know you'll work for free! And what of Mitrofin's daughter? You did a world of good there. You built an entire carriage for her in a month, but she went to Gregory's side because he gave her black tea and shiny white pearls.

You fool! Do what they want, not what you think they need!

And so, Sergei, it is time. Now…nobody will clean YOUR stalls or throw hay to YOUR pony. Nobody will water or weed YOUR garden. Why Olga would be the only one to wash your clothes, yet she found fault in you too—for what you never cared to know.

Yes, Sergei, it is time. The river flows faster and farther away each day. Your blood is spilling everywhere, for nothing. Save yourself lad! I mean YOURSELF! Sergei!

Now go! Do as I say just once. Sergei, listen to ME! I will tell you the truth about yourself. AFTER ALL, I AM YOU!

9-10-01

Something Out of Nothing

So from where does man get this odd idea that you need the right tools to build something, the financial means to start something, or the artistic genius to create a masterpiece? Well?...

Well, once upon a time there was a fine, tall man of about thirty. And without going into proper detail about his background (only for the sake of saving his family name from ridicule and banishment), I will call our hero, Mr. N.

Mr. N. was a polite, responsible, and dear fellow. He always addressed the ladies in a courtly manner, always treated the gentlemen with honorable respect, and above all, was always in a positive and jovial mood.

Mr. N. always tried his best at whatever endeavor he took on. Whether it be a game of some sorts, building a room for his house, writing a poem, painting a painting, or just advising his children. He did his best. Nevertheless, he wasn't satisfied because he always fell short of his rival, his brother, or his neighbors. If he built a room, it wasn't big enough. If he played in a game, he was "okay". If he wrote a poem, it was of elementary value only. Subsequently, he never felt good about himself or an equal to others. But show it he never did. He knew he was worth something and he just needed to feel that he was worth something to himself. Well, little did he know that he was about to be shown a lesson he would never forget. And in a very strange way.

About a quarter to ten on a Friday morning, he noticed a long line in front of an unrecognizable "store." Now this wasn't any ordinary store. You see, people were standing in line, but they weren't ordering anything or paying any money for any goods. But they were exiting with items quite unusual for, well, going to the "store." All came out carrying rather large boxes filled with tools and various building materials. The only thing is that each person was given different tools and a mismatch of assorted and, shall we say, "whacky" items: large and small pieces of wood, chunks of bronze, stone bricks, nails, buckets, hammers, glass, and so forth.

Stranger yet was an elderly fellow behind the counter. He was dressed in white overalls, had a white baseball cap on, and sported a white handlebar mustache. In fact, the counter was white, the walls were white, and the floor was white. But looking around there were no signs, no advertising, names, product posters, ordinances, or office hours. Nothing. It was as if this office appeared out of nowhere and for Mr. N, just maybe in the nick of time.

I happened to be walking down the street behind Mr. N. and followed him into the store. I was more than intrigued at not only what was taking place, but also why Mr. N. would venture out of his way to see what was going on. So, I decided to observe the situation. As I did, Mr. N. had reached the counter and it was his turn to receive his goods. No, he did not have the choice of "ordering" anything. Our dear elderly robust counter person simply smiled and handed Mr. N. his box and told him to go to the table in the back of the store, take out the contents of the box, and start building. Mr. N. was confused and inquired, "Build what, sir?"

The kind gentleman responded, "You'll figure it out."

Others had already emptied their boxes onto the counter. One man had several large beams, a door, nails, a hammer, and cement. A lady had a huge stone, bags of cement, a chisel, and a brush. Mr. N. emptied his contents out on the table before him. "Hmm," he mumbled, "looks like I don't have much of anything. What's this?

A hammer, nuts and bolts, a piece of glass, a metal pipe, a square piece of wood, some paint, and a marble. Odd."

He began to look around at the people working. People were hammering, sawing, nailing, cutting, painting, carving, gluing, soldering, and performing half a dozen other construction details. Mr. N. carefully separated his materials, stared at them for several minutes, and, well, began to "build." He started with the wood, put the marble on it, fit the pipe on top, broke the glass into smaller pieces and glued them on the wood, screwed the nuts and bolts through the metal pipe, and painted everything. Feeling somewhat satisfied, he put his hands on his hips, took a couple of steps back, and exclaimed to himself, "WHAT THE HELL IS THAT!"

He noticed the guy next to him had built a beautiful stall for his horse. A woman down the way had made a very elaborate sculpture of a ballet dancer. Mr. N. was quite upset and felt downright stupid, mortified, and humiliated. He turned around and bolted to the counter and confronted the shopkeeper in a rather unorthodox manner for Mr. N. "I say, sir. Damn you! I think there's been some mistake. You gave me nothing to work with. There was nothing in that box that compared to the others'. Why, I wasted my time and felt like an idiot! What am I to do, kind sir? Mine is nothing like the others'."

Just then, as if on cue, the people at the counter stepped aside and the shopkeeper calmly put his hands on the counter, looked at Mr. N. with a broad smile, and simply whispered, "Look again."

As Mr. N. turned, he saw a large crowd of people gathered around his creation. The people at the counter were now rushing to see what he had built. There were "oohs and ahs," "look at this," and "very good." He turned back to the counter and the jolly old fellow had an even bigger grin on his face. He said, "Unique."

Mr. N. was dumbfounded and shot back, "I don't understand what just happened."

"Simple," the shopkeeper began, "YOU MADE SOME-THING OUT OF NOTHING."

Mr. N. turned around. The white mustache man in the white overalls had vanished, as did the store with the white counter, white walls, and white floors.

"To believe you have nothing, are doing nothing, and are nothing is only a mere reflection of a dejected soul. Something is better than nothing! Open your soul."

2001

A Little Girl's Friend

"Oh, please, Miss Meraz, tell us a story! You haven't told us a story for a whole week. We promise we'll be good. Please! We can take our quiz after the story. Please, Miss Meraz!"

All of the seventh graders' pleas were met with a soft smile and a kind expression from the elderly, petite, and still attractive sixty-year-old woman.

"Well, okay, Boys and Girls. But just ONE story, then it's quiz time. And not one, single peep from any of you or I'll have to stop. Is that clear?"

All the students nodded in agreement and said, "Yes, Miss Meraz."

"Then everyone sits in a circle on the floor."

The children did as they were told. When everyone was settled and quiet, Miss Meraz began, "Now, what story do you want to hear? *The Eleventh Jack-O-Lantern*? What about *The Eagle and the Bear*?"

Most of the students were too shy to reply, while some of the more confident ones sighed. But one blue-eyed, blonde-haired girl named Svetlana spoke her mind. "No, Miss Meraz. We've already heard those stories. Tell us a new story. Better yet, what's that brown book on your desk? Read a story from that book. The one with the torn sides and the funny writing on the front cover. It's got a picture of a little girl, a horse, and the sun on it. She's reaching up and hugging the horse. What's that book about?"

Miss Meraz's caring expression suddenly turned to depression. Her eyes immediately fell upon the little brown book that Svetlana was asking about. Miss Meraz felt queasy and her heart began to beat rapidly.

Svetlana asked worriedly, "Miss Meraz, are you okay?"

"Yes, Sveta. I'm okay. But I can't read that book. It's a very special book. It's a whole short story in itself...I really can't read from—"

Svetlana, blurted, "But Miss Meraz, you never even OPEN the book! You take it out when we're working and you stare at the cover, but you never read it."

"I know, Svetlana. I'm sorry. It's special. It's very personal. I..."

As Miss Meraz's voice slowed, then paused, the rest of the children could see tears in her eyes. Several students tried to cheer her up by telling her it was okay. Then quietly, slowly, and purposefully, she placed her frail, wrinkled fingers around the torn binding and gently took the book from the desk. Miss Meraz carefully cradled the old and tattered book in her hands and stared at it as she had done so many times before. After what seemed to be several minutes, she slowly opened the book to the first page.

The children sat stunned, in silence, waiting for something special and unexpected to take place. Miss Meraz began, her voice trembling, "Okay...okay...I...I'll read from the little brown book. It starts like this...

"Once upon a time in the tiny town of Bonsall, near the larger town of Fallbrook, located north of San Diego..." "Hey! Alex! The old, black mare is ready to come off the hot-walker. Bring her in, groom her, and give her mash. And don't forget to put the fish oil on her feet. Understand?"

* * *

Fyoder Ivanovich, Russian immigrant and horse trainer, cut short his barking orders to Alex and began to talk to himself, "Stupid runt. Doesn't have a brain in his head. Not a clue. Can't talk. He can hear fine, but he hasn't muttered a word in the two years that he's been here. Weird. He's ignorant and an idiot to boot. How DID Mother Nature create such a lowly creature? But man, can he work! Does the work of five grooms. He can clean five stalls, groom, tack, and then rebed the stalls for the same five horses, all alone, in less than an hour! Amazing! Well, enough thinking out loud."

Alex Gregory did as he was told. He walked to the hot-walker, turned it off, opened the gate, and walked in. He approached a robust, black, fifteen-year-old thoroughbred mare, named Sunset.

As Alex entered the hot-walker enclosure, the horse side-stepped a little, but when she felt Alex's familiar and comforting hand, she settled down. He reached up, unsnapped the lead rope from the metal arm that held the rope to the automatic walker, and led Sunset to her stall. Once inside, she made several turns, occasionally dropping her head to smell the fresh clean straw. She went over to her hayrack looking for food. And although she knew by habit that nothing would be in it for another thirty minutes, she still sniffed the feeder and the ground around her, hoping to find some morsel left from the morning's feeding. After several loud snorts, she went to the far corner of her 20 x 20 stall and stuck her nose in the automatic water dispenser.

SWOOSH came the familiar sound as she guzzled down three or four large gulps. Then, as if giving her approval, she pranced to the stall door, stuck her head out, and laid it on Alex's shoulder, licking his neck and dripping water all down the side of his face. She began to whinny softly, talking to Alex. Alex reached out gently with his strong powerful hands and rubbed Sunset's head and scratched her nose. Then he brushed Sunset's long, black mane back with his fingers.

The soft whinnying brought an accomplished smile to Alex's face. He patted Sunset on her muzzle and "told" her with his eyes, "I'll miss you."

It was time to get back to work. That ever-present Fyodor would give Alex a tongue lashing if he caught him spending too much time visiting with the horses. Alex gave Sunset a "good-bye" nod then strode off down the shed row.

The racetrack was in full swing. Fyoder was shouting orders to everyone, riders were hurrying to get on their mounts, and Alex was busy once again cleaning stalls, tacking and untacking horses, and cleaning feed tubs.

At about eleven o'clock, right before lunch, the track began to quiet down. The last of the racehorses had left the track, others were being taken off the hot-walkers and being led to their stalls, while the tractors were getting ready to harrow the dirt on the track. The vet had arrived to make his daily rounds, and the horse-shoer was already putting shoes on his fourth horse of the day.

When the shed row had been raked, all the saddles and bridles cleaned and the coffee readied for tomorrow, Alex made his way into his small tack room that served as his "home." It was at the end of the shed row and was actually an empty stall that was made into Alex's sleeping quarters.

Alex slid back the huge iron door, then took one last look down the shed row to see if everything was tidy and ready for tomorrow. Before he stepped inside he glanced at the horses and counted fifteen heads. Satisfied with his morning's work, he stepped inside, walked to the small cot located under the only window, and collapsed from exhaustion. He lay there gazing around his 20x20 room, taking notice of his world: the tiny nightstand, a lamp, a small tray, two changes of clothes, saddles, bridles, an old wooden chest. Before Alex closed his eyes, he did what he always did before going to sleep. He stared at that old wooden chest that sat in the corner and was covered by an old green horse blanket. It could have been any ordinary, old wooden chest with a lock, but it wasn't. On one side, it bore the inscription: Moi Veshchi (My Things). On the other, a date: Dekaber, 15 (December 15). Then the words: *Bolshovo Uspexa, Tebya Lublyu. Dedushka Tvoj* (Good Luck. I Love you. Your Grandfather). Alex sighed heavily, rolled over, and fell asleep for his two-hour nap.

Not more than an hour had passed when Alex was awakened by the shouts of two men arguing. Alex recognized the voice of one man, that being Fyoder's. But the other man was a stranger. Alex got up cautiously and peered out the door. He saw Fyoder arguing with a tall, robust man of about six feet four inches. He had huge shoulders, thick, wavy brown hair, and a thick mustache.

And although the stranger spoke Russian, he had a slight French accent.

"Come on, Fyoder! That mare is finished. She's a waste of money. I can't feel sorry for these horses. They're a business. You owe us a lot of money, Fyoder. She's cash in. She's headed for an 'accident,' then the glue factory. I'm shipping her out tomorrow."

"No!" Fyoder shouted back.

"You can't do this. She will get better. She stays. I'll think of something. You leave! You go now!"

As the man turned to leave and Alex was about to close the door, a little girl suddenly came around the corner of the barn and down the shed row. She walked past the stranger and headed right for Sunset's stall, which was right across from Alex's room. Alex hid behind the iron door and watched the little brown-haired girl as she walked up to Sunset's stall door and fearlessly reached out and touched the black mare on her cold, wet muzzle. Sunset let out a snort, which didn't even cause the little girl to flinch. As she rubbed Sunset's forehead, a woman's voice could be heard from the other side of the barn, "Angelica! Angelica!"

Seeing Angelica petting Sunset, the woman nervously told the little girl, "Angelica, be careful. You'll scare the nice horse and it may bite you."

Confidently, Angelica told her mother, "But, Mommy. She's a nice horse. I can tell. She wouldn't hurt anyone. Look, Mommy, she's licking me. I love her, Mommy. Can she come home with us? Please?"

"No, baby. Now come along."

Just then, Alex emerged from his tack room. He held out his arms and gestured to Angelica. The girl's mother nodded her approval and the little girl was no sooner in Alex's arms and then on Sunset's back. Angelica was so happy she looked into Alex's eyes and said, "Thank you", then asked, "Is she your horse?"

Alex shook his head no.

Angelica continued to rattle off questions to which Alex seemed to understand, yet also ignored. Finally, Angelica asked, "What's the matter, Mister, can't you talk?"

Angelica's mother approached and asked Alex to get Angelica down. She also scolded Angelica for asking so many personal questions. As she reached out for her daughter, her eyes met Alex's. She froze. Then she introduced herself, "Hi. I'm Lisa, Angelica's mother."

Alex nodded politely, yet she could see the frustration on his face, as if he wanted so desperately to say hello and tell her his name. Lisa's beautiful brown eyes were affixed to Alex's as if she had found someone she'd been looking for all her life, but never found. Alex smiled once again. The lady offered her hand again. Alex gently obliged. She shook his hand and softly said, "Thank you, Mister. You're nice. Can I come and see the horse again?"

Alex once again nodded his approval, turned, and walked away.

Lisa took Angelica by the hand and began to leave the barn. As they got halfway down the shed row, Angelica turned around and smiled. Alex had done the same. Their eyes and smiles met.

Lisa met Fyoder in the office and asked about Alex.

"That's Alex. He can't speak. He's my best worker. I don't know anything about him. He wandered in here one day, grabbed a runaway horse, and he's been here ever since. Thing is, he acted as if he knew one horse in particular, the mare, Sunset. He hangs out with her all the time and rides her in the hills after work. Anyway, it's as if he was half horse himself. He understands them so much."

As Fyoder talked, Lisa stared off into space, thinking about Alex, thinking about her marriage to Ivan, the very same "stranger" who had been arguing with Fyoder. Then, out of nowhere, a voice rang out, startling everyone, "Lisa! Bring Angelica and let's go! I saw you talking to that groom. What for? Do I bore you that much that you need to talk to the stable help? Or are you feeling sorry for someone again? My poor wife. I give her everything, but she insists she doesn't know love. Let's go."

A few days passed, then a few weeks. Life at the racetrack was peaceful and routine. Angelica came almost every day to see her new friend, Sunset. She brought carrots and sugar cubes and adorned Sunset's stall door with pictures, roses, and ribbons. They became inseparable. If Angelica were late, Sunset would weave back and forth in her stall, whinnying at the top of her lungs. And after each meeting, Alex would just smile, nod his head, and wave good-bye.

At 4:00 p.m., just when Angelica was saying good-bye to Sunset, all the horses would start rattling their feed tubs, nudging their gates, and splashing in their waterers. Alex had ten minutes to grain fifteen horses. He would then make a final "run," a last cleaning of the stalls, then check all the horses and take Sunset out for a ride in the local foothills. Riding, Alex usually thought about his beloved horses and his own past. His thoughts drifted to Angelica and Lisa. He remembered how their eyes had first met, the kind words she had spoken to him, and the yearning in his heart that he felt for both Lisa and Angelica.

He saw scenes of Angelica petting Sunset's forehead and sitting on Sunset's back. However, thoughts of joy turned to anxiety as images of Ivan entered his head. He began to think, *That Ivan hasn't been around much. I wonder what he is up to?*

Two more weeks passed when Alex was suddenly sent to the city to buy some supplies. This was not his ordinary job, but being the obedient worker he was, he went. Upon returning in the evening to the main gate, Charlie the guard, who was Alex's friend, told Alex that a trailer had arrived about two hours earlier to Fyoder's barn and had picked up three horses.

Horrified, he made a mad dash to the barn, only to find three empty stalls, the last one, Sunset's! He ran to the stable office and found Fyoder sitting in a chair, his head buried in his hands. He looked up and whispered in a sullen voice, "Alex, I'm sorry. I had no choice."

Alex went to the office door and found the shipping order. It read: *Three horses, two three-year-olds and one fifteen-year-old mare. Destination XYZ Farms.*

Alex knew this was the code for an "accident" and ultimately the glue factory.

He grieved the entire night, not only for Sunset, but for Angelica as well. He awoke in the early morning at 2:00 and stood in front of Sunset's stall and wept. Alex felt helpless. He was also angry.

How could Fyoder let this happen? Maybe he was involved with this "stranger"? Maybe he was with the mob. He was here a long time ago talking about insurance money with Fyodor. That's it? The insurance policy was to expire soon and it's worth $100,000 right now.

Alex had seen a copy of this policy in the stable office once. Now everything was very clear to him. It was time to fight back. He began to make plans of his own...

After the morning gallop and the last horse had been taken to its stall, Alex went to the kitchen for his daily bowl of fruit and cup of hot tea. As he was leaving, he was startled by Angelica's sudden presence. There was fear in the little girl's eyes. All Alex could do was force a faint smile of hope. He reached out, hugged Angelica, and looked up at Lisa. Alex picked Angelica up and held her tight. The little girl looked into Alex's eyes and softly reassured him, "It's okay, Alex. It wasn't your fault. You're still my best friend."

Lisa was crying. "Thank you, Alex, for all your kindness. You're a kind man…good-bye. We have to go now." Alex sadly watched as the two of them rushed out the gate to an awaiting Mercedes.

Driving off, Angelica blurted to her mother, "Mommy, I saw where Alex lives."

"You mean you went into his room?"

"No, Mommy. I went to the window, stood on a hay bale, and looked in. There's a big wooden box. It was open and I saw papers and books in it. There was a nightstand and on it was a bunch of pictures of kids. There were papers with funny writing on it. There was also a big picture of Sunset. She was wearing roses."

Lisa was curious but she had no choice but to correct her daughter. "Angelica, promise me that you will never look at someone else's private things again. It's not polite."

"Okay, Mommy."

Lisa wasn't as upset as she was curious. "Books? Papers? Funny Writing?" she began to ask herself. "Who is Alex Grego-ry?"

The next day, Lisa walked down the deserted shed row to Alex's tack room and climbed up the hay bales stacked outside his window. She opened the unlocked window and slipped in. The window was adjacent to a hillside that was maybe five feet away from the tack room. It ran straight up. It was almost impossible for anyone to spot Lisa coming in. They would never have a reason to look in this isolated area.

She located the old, wooden chest with the now barely recognizable Cyrillic alphabet on it. She opened the chest. Her eyes grew bigger and bigger as she surveyed the contents.

"Oh my God!" she began. "Russian! This is Russian! Alex—Alexi, Gregory—Gregoree, in Russian!" She opened a lid that seemed to be covering a secret compartment in the chest. What Lisa saw next, she couldn't believe! Angelica was right! There were pictures of kids in a classroom. And Alex was in front; he was the teacher! He was talking!

Lisa found textbooks in Spanish, Russian, math, history, and science. She found letters from students and evaluations from principals. There were certificates of appreciation from businesses and thank-you cards from exchange students. Lisa was in shock.

Next, she looked under Alex's cot. There were two briefcases. She pulled them out. They were unlocked, so she opened them. In the first one, there was a list. It read: "Titles of short stories by the unknown author, Alexi Gregorovich. Upon death, I ask that these stories be given to the children's library at Marston School, where, for ten years I taught with all my heart and soul and gave my last drop of blood. Until things happened..."

The note stopped abruptly. Lisa found a collection of children's stories about animals, sports, family, travel, and much more. They were all neatly typed and ranged in length from three to thirty pages.

She set one briefcase aside and opened the other one. There was another list entitled, "Poetry, Anecdotes and Thoughts." There were letters in Russian and English as well. Lisa asked herself, "So Alex was once a wonderful teacher and an aspiring writer. What happened?"

The horses began to whinny. Alex was returning. She put everything back, closed the chest, and climbed out the window. She came out into the shed row and visited the horses as if nothing had taken place.

Fyodor walked around the corner as Alex came up the road that led to the barn. "Lisa, what a pleasant surprise. Did you fall in love with the racetrack that fast? Where's Angelica?"

"Well, Fyodor, Lisa began. "It's about Angelica. She's quite concerned. And Ivan won't tell me anything regarding Sunset's whereabouts. It's not fair. So for Angelica's sake, Fyoder, what's going on?"

At first, Fyodor was defiant. "Now, Lisa! It's out of the question. It's business. It was just a matter of time. It was inevitable. She can't pay her keep anymore. She's through racing. She hasn't the best bloodlines, and she's too sore to be an outriding horse. She's worth more in other ways."

"What other ways? The glue factory?" Lisa shouted back. "Fyodor, that mare means everything to Angelica, not to mention Alex's unknown love for her. Isn't there ANYTHING we can do?"

"Look, Lisa, I've lost a lot of money. Most of it went to that mob husband of yours. Now he OWNS me! To think that I let him in my life, trusted him, introduced him to my friend whom he marries, and then, KAPUT! He doesn't come around for weeks. He calls with deals and bets. He shows up here and demands money and threatens me. So is this American capitalism? I'd rather sell the mare, buy a bottle of cheap vodka, a plane ticket, and return to Russia. So, Lisa, I love that damn Sunset more than anyone. But I—"

Fyodor was cut short by the surprise appearance of Alex as he walked around the corner of the barn. Alex pretended to be caught off guard when he saw Lisa. He had been standing in one of the stalls on the other side of the barn, listening to the entire conversation.

He smiled. Lisa forced a soft expression on her face. Fyodor just lowered his head, walked by Alex, and muttered, "Never make these racehorses your friends."

When Lisa arrived at her Del Mar home, she found Ivan watching TV and talking on the phone. She only heard one side of the conversation, "Okay...Lukov, okay! Look...yes...The horses are at the Chris Mar Ranch...Next week...about 100,000 for the mare...About thirty days...good-bye."

Ivan was somewhat startled to see Lisa, but played it down, "Hello, darling. How are you? Angelica is in her room, playing with her Barbies."

Lisa couldn't hold back her frustration, and she began to speak. She didn't notice Angelica was halfway down the stairs when she began to yell at Ivan, "How could you do this to your own daughter? She's only eight years old! You are not the man I married! You've become treacherous. Your so-called friends, as I knew them in the beginning, have turned out to be mobsters them-selves. So, I take it that everything we own has been bought with dirty money? Well, I'm not using any of the money you get for killing a horse that your own daughter loves and cherishes! What is wrong with you? You've become a cold-blooded murderer. I'm through with you!"

Ivan didn't expect Lisa's reaction, but he did have a feeling that she had had enough of his dealings. Feeling at a loss, he let her have it. "What's wrong? Is that wanna-be Russian idiot making you feel sorry for him? We can get ten horses for Angelica when this is all over. C'mon, Lisa! Think about what you have! Think of who you were before you met me!"

"I was poor, I struggled. I had nothing. But I DID have my pride!"

Lisa was furious. She ran upstairs to get Angelica. Angelica had scampered back to her room and was sitting on the floor when her mother came in.

"Angelica! C'mon, baby. We're going to Grandma's for a while."

On the way out the door, Lisa turned to Ivan who was now sitting on the couch, and screamed at him, "How could you, Ivan! How could you! You've made a choice you'll always regret."

Angelica was one of the best students in her second-grade class. Everyone loved her. But today, while the others around her worked, she doodled and stared out the window. Her thoughts drifted to all of the pictures she had drawn of Sunset, Mommy, and Alex. She kept asking herself, "Why?"

Her attention focused on an aging oak tree outside on the playground, its massive trunk, thick branches, and green-brown leaves rustling in the wind.

Angelica began to count the branches. She noticed how some were full of leaves and others were bare, rotten, and looking as if they were hanging uselessly—no good for anything, to anyone, anymore.

Angelica thought, *Maybe the leaves don't want to be on them anymore. Maybe nobody wants to tie a rope to the branch so the kids can swing. So all of the branches just hang there, dying off. And the oak tree is in the corner, alone and sad.*

Angelica's thoughts went from anger to curiosity. *What if a little girl liked one of the old branches? Maybe she'd make a hummingbird feeder and put it on the branch. Or maybe she'd decorate it. The branch might like the little girl too. No matter, the little girl wouldn't let anyone hurt the branch—if she could help it!*

"Angelica. Angelica! The bell rang. Your mom will be mad if you're late."

"Yes, Mrs. Radisson."

"Where's your mind today, child? My! My!"

As Angelica got in the car, Lisa knew something was wrong. "How was recess today, baby?"

"Okay."

Angelica didn't say much. Inside, she wanted to tell her mom, but she was too afraid. "Mommy, if a branch from a tree is too old and someone loved it, would they cut it off and kill it anyway?"

"I don't think so, sweetie. Why?"

Lisa was hurting for Angelica because Angelica really knew the truth.

Angelica began to cry. "Mommy, they're going to kill Sunset for money. I know! I heard Daddy on the phone and I heard you talking to Daddy."

"Angelica, stop! Nobody's going to hurt her. She went away for a while."

"Mommy, you said never to lie about anything!"

Lisa thought for a moment, *She's right.* "You're right, honey! I won't lie, but I won't let anything happen to Sunset. I promise!"

"Thank you, Mommy. I love you!"

"I love you too, princess."

"Maybe Alex can help, Mommy. He loves Sunset so much. And I love Alex. Mommy He's a good man."

Lisa began thinking to herself, *Alex IS* a good man. I made a mistake. I think Alex just may be able to help all of us!

Fyodor paid close attention to Alex this morning. His worst fears were confirmed after only a brief observation. Alex wasn't really working. Rather, he was just going through the motions.

"Alex, you okay? What's the matter with you? You never work this slowly. You ill? Take the day off. Go rest."

Alex didn't even look up. He simply dropped his rake in the very spot where he was working and walked out of the shed row, down the access road, past the entrance to the track, walked out the main gate, got on an old rusty-colored mountain bike, and took off down the dirt road.

Soon after Alex had left, Lisa and Angelica showed up at the barn. Fyodor was hanging up the last of the bridles. Angelica asked him if he would take her to see the new foals in the pasture. Fyodor obliged with a big grin and off they went. As planned, Lisa made sure nobody was watching, then made her way to the back of the barn and to Alex's tack room window. She opened the window and slipped inside. She took the horse blanket off the chest, opened it, moved a few books, and found the stories. And to her astonishment, she found a story entitled, Sunset, a Groom's Best Friend. She wasn't exactly sure what she had in mind, but she put the five-page story into her pocket, closed the chest, put the blanket back, and made her way back out the window, again un-seen. She began to walk to the pasture and as she was walking, she read the story. It told of Alex's hardship and the joy that Sunset had brought to him. The last part caught Lisa's attention. It read:

"Now my journey is almost complete. And after finding Lisa and Angelica, maybe I can return to the life I once had."

Lisa met Fyodor and Angelica at the gate to the pasture.

"Let's go. baby."

"Okay, Mommy."

Angelica walked briskly to her mom, smiling, knowing darn well what had taken place.

Once in the car, Angelica asked, "Mommy, did you find a story?"

"Yes, I did. It's about Sunset. It tells the truth about her life. It also tells about us."

"What does it say?"

"Well, honey…" Lisa wouldn't tell Angelica just yet. "Mommy, we need to do something about Sunset." "I know, dear. We are."

The sun had begun to rise, yet only a crimson band of light appeared suspended above the horizon, silhouetting the empty racetrack against the towering hills toward the west.

Fyodor left the police station, having just told his story. His guilt and grief had been temporarily lifted from his shoulders. He called Lisa and admitted what he had done. She understood. Her husband had turned into a terrible man, and she knew their marriage had been doomed from the start. Her only concern was for Angelica's safety and happiness.

Lisa grabbed Alex's story, got in the car, and drove to the racetrack. It was time to help Alex, save Sunset, and set everyone straight. Lisa had had enough!

It was 2:00 p.m. Angelica was sitting on the floor of her second-grade class. It was story time. Miss Raddison was reading aloud and watching Angelica out of the corner of her eye. She wasn't listening. She was staring out the window. She wore a sad face and her eyes were swollen and red from crying.

Miss Raddison read on. Suddenly, Angelica's eyes grew wide open. She picked her head up, leaped to her feet, and ran to the window, shouting, "Alex! Alex! Alex is here!"

Miss Raddison was startled and puzzled at first, but allowed Angelica to continue.

"Miss Radisson. This is my friend, Alex. He's going to save Sunset. He's Sunset's papa!"

Miss Radisson was too stunned to speak. She looked out the window and saw Lisa, accompanied by a young man, and heading for the classroom. She was confused, but felt that this was much more important than the story she was reading.

"Very well, Angelica, introduce your friend to us."

Lisa and Alex entered and Angelica proudly announced. "Everyone, this is my friend Alex. This is Sunset's daddy. He is going to save her. Aren't you, Alex? Alex can't talk, so you'll…"

Just then, Alex put his hand on Angelica's shoulder. Their eyes met. They smiled at each other. And as if Angelica hadn't been through enough, heard Alex tell her, "It's okay, princess. Everything is going to be okay now."

"Alex, you can talk! You can talk!"

Alex took a worn-out manuscript from his torn coat pocket. He asked the children if they wanted to hear a story. He looked at Miss Radisson. She nodded her approval and Alex began to read aloud, in a strong voice. Both Lisa and Angelica held each other and began to cry.

"Once upon a time, there was a beautiful baby horse. And since she was born at sunset, we gave her the name, Sunset…"

Alex told the story of how they had spent most of their lives together and shared most of the sorrows and joys of their experiences. Alex had been a teacher and had lost a wife and little girl. He quit teaching and took Sunset to the racetrack. She had won the Kentucky Derby and was one of the best racehorses in the country. But she had injured her leg, and the trainers and owners were going to put her to sleep and collect the insurance money.

Well, Alex took all of his savings and used it to fix Sunset's leg and to pay for all of her board and care. When Alex ran out of money, he begged Fyodor to take them in. You see, Fyodor knew about Alex all along! But he had to try and protect Alex and Sunset. All the while, for ten years, Alex wrote stories and dreamed of being a writer, but what he really wanted to do was to teach again. He always pretended that he couldn't talk because he wanted to keep everything a secret.

"So, Boys and Girls, I had no money to keep Sunset. I had lost my teaching job. I took Sunset to the racetrack to be with her and became a groom. And I promised Sunset that I would never leave her. I've kept that promise. Also, I have found two beautiful friends who I will cherish forever."

Alex stopped and looked at Angelica. "And so, my little princess, we won't let anything happen to Sunset. We will save her, just as you and your mother saved me. Lisa, thank you for all of the wonderful things that you have shown me in life. I will teach again; I will write. Maybe we can all be together, even if I have to sleep in the tack room across from Sunset."

Lisa smiled at Alex, hugged Angelica, and began to cry. All the children cheered.

A year has passed since Alex told his story. Since that time, Lisa's ex-husband has been sent to jail, Fyodor became a blacksmith (living in the tack room I might add), and Alex? Well, he's not only teaching and writing, but also giving horseback riding lessons with Sunset. And Alex isn't sleeping in the tack room anymore. Lisa and Angelica wouldn't let him…

* * *

Miss Angelica Meraz, closed the old brown book and told her students, "It's time to take your quiz."

The Last Nail

It is very simple. You take a nail and hold it between the index finger and thumb of your left hand (against that which you are going to strike the nail). Next, you grasp the hammer in your right hand, much the same way you would hold a stick, only this time, harder. Gripping the handle tightly, you bring the head of the hammer crashing down, full force upon the head of the nail.

At this precise moment, you reveal to yourself what all men want to know—if you are indeed weak or strong. Yes, there are always circumstances. Some would venture to argue that some hammers require only one or two swift and powerful blows to drive the nail straight through a two-by-four, while still others would contend that some hammers require four or five choppy, delicate taps to accomplish the same feat. But suppose it was not this easy. Suppose neither the strong person nor the weak person could pound our innocent piece of steel (no matter what hammer they used!) into its designated destination? What if the nail simply refused to even enter the board, let alone go through it?

I cannot speak for you, but I would become quite upset. I would commence to beat the nail's head senselessly with the hammer, any hammer. Or even smash it with all my might using a lumber mallet or stoker's implement.

At this time I need to point out to the reader that my objective is not to confuse, embarrass, or mislead you in any way. It is to reveal to you that just such a case did take place some fifty years ago around the time of the revolution, when all the nails were being driven into wood by all of Peter the Great's carpenters.

That is to say, except for one old rusty nail. It was one of the last nails found after the carpenters were ordered to gather up the remaining pointed objects, put them into a large wooden box, and carefully save them for the final phase of a housing construction project in the city of L., Russia, located some thirty kilometers from St. Petersburg.

You see, up to this point, almost all the steel, iron, and other nails had been used. However, there were still a few, "stray," "rebels" still lurking about. These old, rusty "heroes" were actually left over from the days when people built their homes wherever they wanted to, and, I might add, from the best materials that could be found.

Now, as I was saying, except for one old rusty nail that would not succumb to the great hammer's devastating blows. After being driven halfway in, it stopped and simply refused to go in any farther. Hundreds of thousands of laborers, apprentices, and journeymen carpenters came from all around, and using a varied assortment of hammers and mallets, tried their best, to "finish" the old "hero" off. But it was all to no avail. Nobody, no matter how hard they tried, could drive the nail through the two-by-four that was to hold the frame together.

Next, the chief minister of buildings himself arrived from the city of M. to see what all the fuss was about. "How could a nail cause such a stir?" he asked himself. But after witnessing the stubbornness himself, he declared to all, "No nail whatsoever—steel, nor iron, for that matter—shall impede the progress of His Majesty the Tsar's carpenters! I could have this nail and this board thrown into the scrap pile or tossed into the river Neva, but instead, I will prove to you that the progress of the contractors and carpenters of the construction housing project of the city of L. shall not be hampered nor impeded in any way!"

With that, a mighty cheer went up and another thousand men tried, but still failed to pound the nail in. In frustration, the minister then replied to the masses, "To expedite the matter, we shall remove this nail and we will insert the old-style wooden plug in its place."

The crowd was perplexed, but one by one the carpenters now tried to extract the nail, but with the same result; it wouldn't budge!

Morally defeated and feeling very humiliated, the chief inspector announced that he was leaving. All the brave carpenters and men were stunned and also very dejected. They were very mad at the example set forth by their leader. How could he give up in the name of progress!

When all seemed lost, a blue-eyed little girl of eight walked up to the two-by-four, gently touched it with her soft pink hand, then held the nail with her fingers. She then whispered something that only the nail could hear and understand. Suddenly, to the dismay of all who looked on, the little girl carefully tugged and the nail came out easily.

One of the carpenters asked, "What did you say to the nail?"

"I told him he was a true hero and that I promised he could be free. That's all he wanted—was to be free. I promised I would set it free from the wood forever, and it said, 'Okay.'"

* * *

The last house in the project was never finished and the uncompleted skeleton frame still stands alone. No new buildings were ever built in the city of L. The little girl took the nail home and put it on her windowsill, where it is to this day, joyfully soaking up the morning sun.

1986

CONTRARY OPINION

Hello, my name is Contrary Opinion. I was born on a small ranch, not far from the famous San Luis Rey Downs racetrack. There was my mother, father, and myself.

My mother, My Opinion, was a housewife, dedicated to her family. To others, she was noted for her stubbornness as well as her vivaciousness. But to me, she meant love and security. She followed me everywhere, always making me feel as if I was someone or something very special.

My father, All Opinion, on the other hand, was very boisterous and had a bad temper. He was also very wealthy, earning almost $500,000 a year at the racetrack.

He went to the racetrack every day, and came home late in the evening. Sometimes he went away for three or four months at a time, only to return exhausted, undernourished, and oftentimes near death.

Our ranch was on a twenty-acre parcel stretching from the edge of Old Lilac Road all the way to the San Luis Rey River bottom. We lived in a red brick colonial-style mansion, with three large rooms and high wooden ceilings.

There were lush, green pastures in which I ran in for hours on end, while my mother stood next to the redwood fence and talked to the neighbors.

When it was time for lunch, Mom would call me to come inside. Fearing that she would leave me behind, I always ran as fast as I could to her side.

Once inside, I first enjoyed a hearty nutritious meal, topped off with warm milk. Then, it was time for my afternoon nap. I'd lie down and snuggle up to my mother until it was time for supper.

When my father was home, he saw to it that everything on the ranch was in proper order. He conferred with the grooms, making sure all the horses on the ranch were being properly cared for. At night, he walked the darkened perimeter, ensuring that no prowlers or loose animals were lurking about.

Sometimes, on crisp, clear mornings, Mother and Father went for long walks in the eucalyptus groves. There, they discussed the past and made plans for the future.

* * *

Recently the Del Mar racing season came to a close. But as always, my mother and I were very happy during Del Mar because the racetrack was only twenty miles away, and this meant that we could spend more time together as a family.

However, just before the end of this year's racing program, tragedy struck at home.

On the last Monday morning of the meet, my father left for the racetrack at the usual hour of 5:00 a.m. However, when he was leaving, I overheard my parents arguing from an adjacent room. I only heard part of their quarrel, which went something like, "Please quit! You're pushing yourself too much! I love you.

But you never know when to quit. You'll die young if you don't quit now. Please! Please! I love you! They will kill you." My father's voice was gentle toward my mother, but stern. "I am committed. I have no choice. I cannot quit. I can only survive. Good-bye. I will be home after supper. Take care of Contrary for me."

Later that day, Mother and I were walking near the riverbank. She was unusually silent, and when I asked her what she and Father had been discussing that same morning, she only replied, "Oh, there is a very big race today. It is very important and means a great deal to the family's security and to your father's reputation."

On our way inside I noticed two grooms putting away three large syringes in a medicine cabinet. I asked Mother what they were for.

"Nothing!" she snapped.

I stared at her until she finally continued, "It's none of your business. But remember, have fun while you are young. Do what you want to do now, for someday you may be compelled to do things in life that will not only hurt you but also hurt those you love as well."

"But why do we do them?" I asked. "To SURVIVE!" she yelled back.

Later that afternoon, I awoke from my midday nap only to find my mother standing in a corner of the room, staring off into space. She seemed very sad. I tried to cheer her up, but it was to no avail.

A few hours later, a large horse van pulled up in front of the house. I saw the vet, Dr. De Paul, the groom, Señor Alfredo; and our landlord and our very own uncle, Mr. Monwell. All three exited the cab and rushed to the rear of the van. As I turned to tell my mother to come to the window, I noticed she was already standing with her nose up against the window panes, sobbing uncontrollably. Then, she screamed, "OH GOD! NO! NO!"

Next, the three men opened the rear door, went inside, and affixed a rope to a pair of shoes that protruded from the rear of the trailer.

Curiously, I watched as the three men began to pull with all their strength. A few moments later I stood dumbfounded as they proceeded to pull the lifeless carcass of a massive, two thousand-pound thoroughbred racehorse onto the ground. I was horrified. I couldn't run, I couldn't cry. I was too scared to move.

"Don't look!" I heard my mother yell from what seemed a thousand miles away. I was paralyzed by the sight of what was before me...

"Turn away, damn you!" my mother yelled again.

There he was lying on his side, all four of his once-powerful legs, hanging limp, his always-fiery eyes, cold white, his proud head tilted to one side, his cold muzzle partly covered in the sand and blood oozing from his mouth.

This is the last time I saw my father. "Why?" I asked myself.

I repeated what my mother had told me, "To survive. To survive."

The Eleventh Jack-o'-Lantern

Good morning, Mr. Thomas. And just how are you on this beautiful morning?"

"I'm fine, sir. Just joyously fine, Mr. Nichols. How might you be today?"

"Oh fine and dandy, thank you."

"Then, Mr. Nichols, all is fine, everyone is fine, fine, fine..."

Little, plump, red-faced Mr. Nichols, an unpleasant sort of fellow, was always running around clad in blue-denim overalls, a red cowboy shirt, steel-toed boots, and a broom in his left hand. Unpleasant because he carried an old, filthy ragged, god-forsaken handkerchief in his right hand, one which he would continuously blow his nose into.

Poor old man. Seventy-four years old yesterday, the day before Halloween. Lost his wife a couple of years ago to a witches' brew. Now he spends his days caring for Mr. Thomas's garden and sipping on the homemade sauce himself.

"Mr. Thomas, sir, it is Halloween tomorrow and I was wondering if Your Honor would be so kind as to allow me to have ten pumpkins from Your Honor's pumpkin patch?"

Mr. Thomas began to think contemptuously. *Mr. Nichols is a bothersome old fool. He's always asking for some little trifle or another. He sure knows how to get things out of people though.*

Begrudgingly, Mr. Thomas turned to Mr. Nichols and replied, "Take them, you scoundrel! But tell me, what on earth do you want with TEN pumpkins? Could not ONE, or TWO suffice? Besides, aren't you a little old to be carving out jack-o'-lanterns?" The reader should now be fully introduced to Mr. Thomas, his very character, and Mr. Nichols' motive behind the ten pumpkins…

Your Honor, a district court judge, six feet, sixty years old, and owner of sixty acres. A skinny old malicious, evil man who spends nothing on anyone, or on anything for that matter. He sits at home and contemplates the sentencing of his prisoners. Yes, a true, scornful, ancient old geek who year after year denies the charities, the people, and the entire world of any goodwill.

Last year, Mr. Nichols approached the front porch with a request from the neighborhood children. The kids wanted some of the judge's old clothes—some robes—for a Halloween party. But they were just too frightened to ask the judge themselves. So, they asked Mr. Nichols to ask for them. Mr. Nichols obliged the children, but it was to no avail. Mr. Thomas responded by standing on the front porch and screaming at the top of his lungs.

"All a man has are the clothes on his back! Go buy your own clothes! Furthermore, don't come around here for any treats. You'll get nothing from me!"

Mr. Nichols awoke at 4:00 a.m. this Halloween morning, donned his familiar overalls and boots, stuffed the same used handkerchief into the top pocket, left the warm confides of his one room studio, and headed out down the darkened foggy trail that led to the pumpkin patch. Once there, he cut ten, skull-sized pumpkins, then placed them carefully into a small wooden cart and took them back to his studio.

Once inside, he pulled out several pictures he had of Mr. Thomas, each showing off a different face and mood. He studied these immoral features thoroughly for a few minutes, then he took out a carving knife that he had taken from his master's kitchen and began to carve. He carefully etched out the pumpkins with exact likenesses of the old judge's face.

Ten pumpkins, ten faces, each depicting the various sinful and violent moods of Mr. Thomas. When completed, they would tell the complete, true story of a very despicable and hateful man— well, almost the complete story…

The first pumpkin showed the pudgy-nosed face, the short ears, the large eyeteeth, and the terse lips. The second pumpkin had the old man in a fit of rage, his eyes screwed up and his mouth contorted. On and on Mr. Nichols carved until…

At exactly an hour before the judge returned from town, Mr. Nichols placed all the jack-o'-lanterns throughout the house on the windowsills. They burned brightly, burned true and each told its story.

Mr. Thomas soon returned home and took sight of his new decorations and flew into a fit of rage. And when he saw Mr. Nichols standing in the hallway grinning at him, he began to yell, "This is your doing, you old fool! I'll do away with you! You're finished here! Always sorry for people! You're an idiot! Get out!"

Mr. Nichols started to walk toward Mr. Thomas. He drew nearer, then calmly replied, "You are correct, sir. I am everything and even more that you accuse me of. But since you are sending me packing, please may I ask just one more thing of you, sir?"

Stunned, Mr. Thomas glared at Mr. Nichols and exclaimed, "What is it, you crazy fool?"

"I need one more jack-o'-lantern!"

And with that, Mr. Nichols revealed the knife that he used to carve the pumpkins with, and -plunged it into the judge's heart!

* * *

Mr. Nichols stood on the doorstep, inviting the children.

"Come in, children. Mr. Thomas welcomes you to his first ever Halloween party! Isn't Mr. Thomas nice to do this, children? Come in please. Plenty of treats for everyone. Now, be good..."

As the children entered the house, they found in each room a jack-o'-lantern, each to the likeness of Mr. Thomas. The children were thrilled and had a marvelous time. They sang songs, danced, and drank cider.

As they were leaving, one little girl looked up at Mr. Nichols and asked, "Where is Mr. Thomas?"

Mr. Nichols replied with a wide smile, "He's all around you." The little girl asked, "but where?"

"Right here," Mr. Nichols answered, as he grinned even more and handed out candy from an eleventh jack-o'-lantern.

TRICK OR TREAT!

1985

HASTE MAKES WASTE

Mr. Whitley was a very prominent old fellow who lived in the township of Littleton, a small community located in a still smaller part of the smallest state, Smally, named, as one would expect, for its state of "smallness."

And that is all very well indeed, but it really has no bearing on our story, or on Mr. Whitley for that matter.

As I was saying, Mr. Whitley, at five feet six inches tall, blue eyes, gray hair, a bumpy nose, elongated ears, a crooked smile, and an enormous dimple on his chin was, shall we say, not your average person.

One Friday after working very hard on his latest novel, Mr. Whitley suddenly remembered a dinner date he had made for that same evening. He also recalled that he had worn the last of his clean undergarments that very day, which now created a slight problem; no clean underwear to dawn.

Frustrated, Mr. Whitley frantically gathered the entire week's laundry, crammed it into the hamper, took a roll of quarters from the change drawer, grabbed a cup of soap, and, being very careful not to upend his precious collectables, headed for the laundry room on the ground floor of his apartment building.

Once there, he placed each item in the washer, neatly distributing the pieces around the center, ensuring a "balanced" load. Having accomplished this, our little friend poured the granulated detergent into the machine.

Whitley closed the lid, inserted the quarters in their respective slots, and pushed the lever forward. He then exited the laundry room and returned to his apartment, turned on the TV, and began to wait twenty minutes for the wash cycle to complete.

The news was the same this Friday, as it had been on all the previous Fridays—theft, murder, plane crashes, terror attacks, budget crisis, and politics. It was so depressing and so so boring. But as Mr. Whitley became enthralled with all these boring topics, he suddenly remembered something very important; HE DIDN'T HAVE A DIME!

Now you might not think that a dime, the news, and a light beer would at all be a proper trio, but when it came to drying some much-needed *chones*, it turned out to be the most important news of the night.

He searched and searched his entire apartment, but he couldn't find a dime. And with two hours to go before dinner, Whitley was becoming, well, shall we say, PANICKED!

Why our dear little fellow was on the verge of a nervous breakdown. All sorts of thoughts were entering his head: *I could run down to the market and ask for change…no, not enough time…. I could simply knock on every door and ask to borrow a dime….Or I could simply* **NOT** *wear any skivvies at all! No, not an option.*

Next, his demonic thoughts turned to the most depressive outcome of all; perhaps he could not attend the $1000-a-plate affair because he WAS NOT WEARING ANY UNDERWEAR!

Why, he'd be the laughing stock of the town. He could just hear people talking about him, *"Poor old chap; couldn't attend because he had no skivvies to wear! Oh dear me!"*

Clad only in his bathrobe he exited his apartment and went to all his neighbors and asked if any of them might have a dime he could borrow. Disaster! Nobody had a single dime to lend. Plenty of people had quarters, nickels, and pennies, but there wasn't a soul who had in their possession a mere dime. You see, all the other tenants had done their laundry earlier in the day and had already used all their dimes!

"*What am I to do?*" Whitley asked himself. He had no choice. He would have to make his way to the market and get change. So off he went.

Astonishing as it is, the clerk at the corner market was completely out of dimes himself, explaining in a pitiful tone to Whitley, "I am sorry, Mr. Whitley, but all the tenants in your complex rid me of all my dimes this morning to do their laundry. I do have plenty of quarters, nickels, and pennies, sir."

Agonizing, Whitley shot back, "I'm doing my laundry too!"

This only brought a blank stare from our helpless clerk and a last comment. "Mr. Whitley, I do LOVE the color of your robe, sir!" With that, our embarrassed dear little lad ran out of the store as fast as he could!

Whitley was in a sad, delirious state. He began to wander the streets, asking strangers for a dime. People began to shy away from him as if he were a madman. He walked all over Littleton, asking out loud, "Does anyone have a dime?"

His mind began to ramble as he became more desperate. There was one hour left before he had to go to dinner. What was he left to do? He was now really depressed and began to feel quite sorry for himself, commenting on how it just wasn't fair.

"Why me? Always happens to me. Something happens. Either I have one brown sock and one green sock, a stain on my shirt, or a pimple on my forehead, not to mention cutting myself shaving, saying something stupid in the presence of high society people, or…it doesn't matter. Whatever WILL happen WILL inevitably happen to me!"

Then, Whitley had an idea. He would go to the police station! Yes! The constable would surely have a dime! Two more blocks to the station and then eight blocks back home. If he ran the entire way, he could just make it. It was worth a try. He HAD to try! It had taken Whitley three months before he got the courage to ask Clair out on a date. It was the most important night of his life.

He arrived at the police station out of breath and barely able to utter those now famous words, "Officer, do you have a dime?" The sergeant at the counter looked up from the iPad he was gazing at without batting an eye and inquired, "Yes, sir. May I help you, sir?"

"Officer, do you have a dime? I was doing laundry and I went to dry my clothes and suddenly realized that I—"

Our puzzled, yet inquisitive young officer stopped Whitley short, "Get to the part about the bathrobe, mister. I can't wait."

Almost in tears by this time, Whitley started to ramble, "Well, Officer, I have a dinner date and I panicked not having a dime to dry my clothes, and I just ran out of the...oh Officer, please! Can you please help me!"

Stern faced, the officer looked Whitley sharp in the eye and replied, "Sure, Mack. I sure will help you."

And with that, Whitley was seized by two uniformed officers and carted off to a cell. He was booked and charged with indecent exposure, disturbing the peace, and well, for being a danger to the public.

Our dear hero spent the night in jail. In the morning he was arraigned. The judge, feeling sorry for him I suppose, dismissed the charges and let Whitley go home.

Tired and drained, Mr. Whitley could hardly walk the eight blocks back to his apartment without stumbling every several feet. Once there he made his way down to the laundry room. As he stepped inside, he found to his astonishment his clothes neatly folded sitting atop the dryer with a note affixed to, of all items, his undershorts. The note was from Clair and it read:

Dear Mr. Whitley,

I am so sorry to have missed you. I found a dime in your pants pocket and after several failed attempts to locate you, I took it upon myself to finish your laundry for you. I hope you don't mind. I can't wait to go out with you. How about next Friday?

Clair
I say, does anybody have a dime?

The Last Rights

I had forgotten my hammer earlier in the day and returned to the housing project around midnight to recover it. I had driven from my apartment on 49th St. in San Diego, to Valencia St. in National City. When I arrived I turned into a makeshift dirt parking lot, parked, and got out of my Nissan 4x4. I proceeded toward the chain-link fence that surrounded the construction site. As I approached the gate that was partly ajar and latched loosely with a piece of chain and an old Masterlock, I began to feel a bit of anxiety and apprehension. This was due in part that it wasn't a normal working hour, and the words from the warning sign posted on the front of the gate stated:

"DANGER! HAZARDOUS AREA. KEEP OUT! VIOLATORS WILL BE PROSECUTED"

The sign has always been there, and yet tonight I really read it as if it was talking to me. Was I a violator? No. I worked here. A laborer, who simply forgot his hammer, was afraid that someone might steal it, and in a state of panic, awoke at 11:15 pm and drove twenty miles to retrieve it. No crime was committed.

The night was pitch black. A soft blanket of dew covered the wooden frame houses and the piles of scrap wood lined the streets. There were new stacks of two-by-fours, one-by-sixes, four-by-fours, and two-by-tens, all neatly placed in their respective places, awaiting to be summoned. One could still smell the fresh scent of Oregon pine, California oak, and Douglas fir.

I felt the nails under my feet as I walked down the street and approached the last house where I had left my hammer. Something though, was amiss, very odd. The usual, "temporary" beams that the plum and line crew installed in order to keep frames aligned until the roof is nailed down were missing! Thirty-two-by-fours, fourteen and sixteen feet long, had disappeared! Not thrown about or broken up by vandals, but missing entirely! How could the frames remain standing? There were not enough nails shot into the cement foundation to keep them from toppling. What was happening? Where could large pieces of lumber "run" off to?

Next, I walked behind the house and noticed that a scrap pile of wood that I had, that very day, stacked—also missing. Maybe someone had carted it off in a wheelbarrow, or kids had thrown it about or down below in the canyon. I better check, I thought.

I walked to the backyard and looked in the vacant lots and down the hill. But nothing. Suddenly I almost fainted! Two houses down in back, two-by-fours, twenty of them, were standing upright walking somberly in a circle! In the middle of this "procession" were scraps and bits of pieces of wood being cremated in a fire. God, I thought, I've gone mad! But no. The boards WERE walking, chanting, "Ashes to ashes, dust to dust…"

It was nothing less than a ceremony for the "DEAD"!

I began to shake uncontrollably. I ran back to the house where I thought my hammer was, searched frantically for a few seconds, then ran as fast as I could toward the front gate.

As I ran, my heart pounded, I began to sweat, and I felt numb all over. Suddenly, every piece of wood in every house was chanting louder and louder, "ASHES TO ASHES, DUST TO DUST!"

I ran faster not looking back. Finally, I reached the front gate. I slipped through and, feeling a sign of relief, a place of safety, turned around only to witness what was by now, a huge bonfire, dancing two-by-fours, and chanting beams.

Taking a deep breath, I turned around and headed for my truck. Then, as if by magic, everything fell silent, the fire ceased to exist, and the dancing boards became motionless.

I was stunned. I fumbled for my keys and as I found the door key and inserted it, I looked up toward the gate. As I did, a huge object smashed up against it. I went to the gate and reached down—my hammer!

---NEXT DAY---

"Look, Joe. The damn homeless were here last night stealing wood again. And they had another fire in here. I thought we had a security guard here."

"We did. But he quit." SO DID I!...

Another World

A long time ago...

It was a spectacular Sunday morning. The wind whistled softly as it swept down the mountain slopes and the air was filled with the invigorating scent of pine and wild licorice. Newborn blades of grass were magnified by tiny dew drops that had settled there during the night. Sparrows chirped and black crows squawked while the sun pulled itself up higher and higher on the horizon.

Tucked away in a small clearing of these lively woods stood a sizable two-story red brick home surrounded by a white lattice fence and a six-foot hibiscus hedge, which discouraged unwelcome visitors from satisfying their curiosity. Beyond the grand house, a herd of chestnut horses grazed on a grassy field and nickered to one another as they ate.

At thirty-eight, Thomas Steinburn was a successful millionaire who took great pride in his beautiful, secluded residence. But, of course, Thomas had many other possessions he valued more dearly than his "cottage in the woods." He had spent a good portion of his five-million-dollar inheritance on race horses, cattle, real estate investments, oil fields, and gambling casinos.

Mr. Steinburn had awakened at his customary 5:00 a.m. sharp on this lovely "day of rest." Bouncing out of bed, he yawned loudly and strode to the closet in search of an exercise suit. He chose to wear the navy blue cotton sweats, donning them quickly in eager anticipation of his daily routine. He began with a hundred sit-ups, fifty knee bends, thirty stretches, and eighty push-ups. As he performed the last ten push-ups, Thomas concentrated on the rhythmic pounding of his heart, the whoosh of air being expelled from his lungs, and the creak of the wooden floor beneath his sweaty palms.

Mr. Steinburn finished up his workout with a five-mile jog around his estate. Satisfied he had pushed himself "to the limit," Thomas headed for the shower. He quickly pulled off his damp, salty garments and threw open the shower door, making it crash loudly against the wall. After stepping inside, he shoved the stained-glass door shut in the same manner. He gave a sharp pull on the golden faucet and began to relax as he felt the warm, soothing water run down his body. He listened intently to the mesmerizing sound of the powerful water jets beating down on the hand-crafted tiles beneath his feet.

It was ten o'clock when Thomas finally sat down for breakfast. He was glad to slurp down freshly squeezed orange juice and munch on Grape Nuts and milk. Saturday's mail was strewn across the table, so Mr. Steinburn decided to sort it out. Scanning the various envelopes, Thomas spotted one from his brother Bill. He ripped it open and pulled out a donation form for Muscular Dystrophy and a handwritten note which said, "Please, Thomas, help us fight MD! I know you can spare a little! Drop Jan and me a line once in a while, will you? Love, Bill." Thomas heaved a sigh and grumbled, "Charities! They want this, that, and even more! I can't even pay my phone bill without giving $1.00 to the Deaf and Dumb. It's ridiculous!" Mr. Steinburn crumpled up the request and tossed it into the wastebasket.

Thomas was getting bored, so he decided to drive into the city and browse through the stores in the big mall. He jogged upstairs and dressed in an expensive gray, pin-striped suit, maroon silk tie, and matching eel-skin shoes. A dash of Polo, a glance in the mirror, and THE Thomas Steinburn was ready to go to town and

SPEND MONEY. He slipped his gold American Express card into his breast pocket, grabbed his leather, diamond-studded key case, and skipped down to the garage.

Thomas felt the adrenaline surging through him as he clicked the garage door opener. "There's my baby," he said softly as his new, forest-green Porsche 989 came into view. He carefully unlocked the door and sat down on the plush sheepskin-covered seat. His eyes stared in wonder at the myriad of electronic dials and gauges, and Thomas began to imagine that he was about to pilot a concorde jet to some distant, exciting place. Four chimes brought him out of the dream before a woman's seductive voice warned him that the door was open. He closed it quickly and shoved the key into the ignition. Vroom! Twelve cylinders hummed powerfully as Thomas pressed his foot lightly on the accelerator. He deftly put the Porsche in reverse and backed out of the garage. Mr. Steinburn then simultaneously depressed the garage door box button and turned the FM stereo knob to the "on" position. Thomas roared out of the driveway in first gear, letting the engine whine until it reached the right RPM to shift into second. He punched the button that corresponded to his favorite rock station and sat back in anticipation. But there was no music. Thomas reached down without taking his eyes off the road and turned up the volume. Still, no sound came from his Jensen quad speakers.

"Damn radio!" Thomas shoved the Porsche into third and flipped the dial back and forth frantically. Not one note could be heard. He snapped the switch off angrily. He would get the radio fixed Monday morning, first thing. In the meantime, Thomas would go to the Warehouse and buy as many CDs as he could get his hands on. After all, his home was filled with the finest stereo equipment that money could buy.

Thomas felt that something was wrong as he pulled into the parking lot of the shopping mall. The people he passed in other cars kept turning their heads rapidly, acting abnormally cautious. He knew he would feel better when he started to spend a little money.

He guided the Porsche into one of the underground parking spaces. He stepped out gracefully and ascended the stairs that led to the mall shops above. As he reached the top of the steps, Thomas felt a strange pang of fear in his chest. He noticed that there were many people around, but he felt quite alone among them. In fact, there was something very odd about these people. They were making weird gestures with their hands and fingers and making grotesque faces at one another. Yet, no one was talking. Or, at least, it seemed that way. Shrugging his shoulders in confusion, Thomas set out for The Warehouse. But when he arrived at the location where the store should have been, instead, he found a candy shop. "They must have moved it somewhere else!" Thomas was getting a little annoyed. He checked his location in the mall at a nearby directory. He was shocked to see that there was no Warehouse listed. He scanned the names again, looking for another store of the same type. Yet, to his astonishment, there were no music or record stores on the list!

He decided to ask a passerby, an elderly gentleman about sixty, frail, and using a cane to walk with. He had a long, white beard and thick, gray eyebrows. As Thomas turned to inquire about the music store, the old man suddenly threw up his right hand and moved his fingers, while at the same time making a very offensive facial gesture. Mr. Steinburn was so embarrassed that he lowered his head and quickly walked in the opposite direction. Poor old guy, he thought, *must be deaf.* THAT'S IT! *They've brought the deaf people here today.* OH, CHRIST! He made another attempt by asking a small, blonde-haired, blue-eyed girl of about thirteen, "Please, can you tell me where the nearest music store is?" The girl's face became red, her expression was blank, and the strange sounds she produced only provided Thomas with the same answer, the same desolate feeling.

Grimacing, he stomped off to Broadway to look for a much-needed clock radio with a built-in alarm. But after searching each of the three floors, he found only funny clocks with vibrators attached to them. They had tags that read: "ACCU-RATE AWAKENING. SLIP UNDER THE PILLOW. TWO-YEAR GUARANTEE."

Oh, well. I can't seem to get anything done here today, Thomas thought sadly.

Suddenly, Thomas came up with an idea. He would purchase a pair of tickets to the upcoming Tina Turner concert. After standing twenty-five minutes in line, while deaf people signed to each other, Mr. Steinburn finally reached the ticket window. He read the sign overhead for prices and the time of the concert, but, oddly enough, only a circus, a baseball game, and a rodeo were listed. "Maybe the concert is already sold out," Thomas muttered despairingly under his breath. He approached the window and asked the red-headed woman behind the counter. "Is the Tina Turner concert sold out?" The woman squinted at him and sent out an elaborate cryptic message with her hands and fingers. Oh no! thought Thomas, *They have a mute working here. How cruel. How could someone do such a thing?* Thomas quickly pulled out a piece of scrap paper, jotted down his verbal request, and handed it to the startled woman. She, in turn, scribbled a reply on it and slipped it through the small opening in the glass window. Mr. Steinburn grabbed it and read the words: "What is a concert? Who is Tina Turner?"

Thomas became enraged and shouted, "That's not cute!" He stalked off, heading for the pizzeria at the end of the mall. He needed a couple of beers and some pizza after everything he had been through.

He stepped inside the restaurant and walked to the cooler to select a beer. Picking out a Lowenbrau, Thomas went to the counter to order his lunch. "I'll take this beer and three slices of pepperoni pizza please." But the fat Italian man behind the register was stunned at Thomas's request.

He smiled uneasily and looked Mr. Steinburn in the eyes as if buying time to formulate a reply. Finally, he blurted out, "Me no hearing person." Thomas slowly turned away from the counter and stared at the patrons sitting around him. There was no exchange of words between anyone. Thomas was so stunned that he turned away quickly and left the silent restaurant.

I can't believe this! he thought incredulously. *Everyone I've seen today has been deaf!* Then Thomas remembered that his friend Sally worked in the Buffums store nearby. "I know that she speaks my language!" Mr. Steinburn started walking briskly and in a few minutes' time found himself riding the escalator up to the lingerie department. He spotted Sally behind a rack of panties and bras. She was helping a customer. As he neared the rack, he noticed that Sally was not conversing with the other woman; she was signing! Thomas approached the two women and exclaimed, "Wow! I didn't know you knew sign language, Sal! Where did you learn that?" The young woman blinked her eyes and squinted at Thomas in confusion. "What's the matter, Sally?" Thomas reached out to grasp her hand, but she recoiled in fear, backing into the clothing rack abruptly. Mr. Steinburn searched Sally's eyes for the friendship they had shared but found no sign of warmth or recognition. "Come on, Sal! This is no way to treat your old buddy from college! Tell me what's wrong!" Thomas crossed his arms and waited for a response. But when Sally began to sign frantically, Mr. Steinburn felt a surge of fright, which propelled him out of the store.

Back outside, Thomas' heart began to beat rapidly and his breath quickened. He had to call someone. He had to tell somebody what had gone on here today. He scanned the area for a phone booth. "Thank God!" Thomas breathed a sigh of relief when he saw a booth only a few feet away. He jogged over to it and reached in his breast pocket for his phone/address book. When he reached for the receiver, Thomas's mouth dropped open and his eyes widened. There was no phone! But there was a teletype machine affixed to a small printer. The keyboard was made up of many unfamiliar two-letter abbreviations. "What the hell is this doing here!" Thomas had screamed loudly but several people passed by the booth without turning their heads. Mr. Steinburn suddenly began to feel sick to his stomach. He broke out in a cold sweat, and his hands started to tremble. He stumbled out of the booth in search of a restroom. But large, black spots began to dance in front of Mr. Steinburn's eyes and he fell to the ground. Thomas pawed at the cement and went into convulsions. The shoppers rushed to assist him. When Thomas looked into their faces they began to sign to him and make horrible noises. He thrashed his arms at the strangers and kicked his legs violently. "Get away from me! Leave me alone!" Thomas lashed out at the people who were trying to help him. Someone had called the paramedics and two big men in white uniforms arrived, grabbed Thomas and strapped him onto a stretcher. Mr. Steinburn struggled to free himself and almost caused the stretcher to turn over. One of the men produced a hypodermic needle and shot a sedative into his arm. They loaded him into the ambulance and motioned to the crowd to move out of the way.

With red and orange lights flashing, the ABCOM unit sped away. Halfway to the hospital the attendant who was seated next to Thomas tapped the driver on the shoulder and signed, "I wonder what it is like to hear? Must be awful. Nobody understands you, like you, or helps you. You can't live a normal life. Poor guy…"

The driver rocked his right fist up and down in agreement.

The Captain and the Admiral

"All ahead full! Man your battle stations! Stand by for incoming enemy aircraft! Zeros at three o'clock!"

"Aye, sir! Man your battle stations!"

"Stand by! Right full rudder, Captain!"

"Aye, Admiral, right full rudder, sir. Standing by."

"On my command, Captain, right full rudder and all ahead full speed."

"Aye, sir."

"Right full rudder! All ahead full! Switch gears, Captain! Now!"

"Switching, sir."

And with this exchange of command, Dad's foot slammed the clutch in while at the same time, I pulled the column gear shift straight down into second gear.

"Order completed, Admiral." "Very well done, Captain."

From here our attention turned toward the hundred Japanese Zeros streaking in from every direction. Perched on my father's lap and gripping the steering wheel, I surveyed the skies in front of us while Dad checked starboard and port while at the same time sipping on his Hamm's beer.

"Stand by to open fire, Captain!" "Aye, Admiral."

"Open fire!"

And with this command, I slid across the old, tan, and battered leather seat of our ancient, embattled green, 57 Ford truck. I began to push and turn every button, knob, lever, and door lock that I could get my hands on.

The battle was full on now. There were planes, cruisers, battleships, and submarines all around us.

"Torpedoes, .50 cals, rockets, and all guns firing, sir!" I yelled.

"Very good, Captain. Now, let's go get that big Japanese battleship, the Goochie- Moochie."

"Aye, sir."

I could see Dad's fifty-year-old expression become very serious. I stared at him and thought, *This is my pop, US Navy WWII pilot and commander—my hero!*

There we were, Dad, sitting cockeyed in the driver's seat, holding on to his Hamm's beer and searching the port side of Highway 8, while I was still sitting in his lap at the helm, searching for the 70th Street escape route. The old Ford truck, its oversized tires whining on the pavement, swayed back and forth in the right lane as we dodged bombs and bullets and tried to maintain our course to the off-ramp.

Just fifteen minutes earlier we had departed our base—Dad's gas station on 40th and University. We arrived at 6:00 a.m. and departed at 3:00 p.m. Upon leaving, we always set out on a different course. Sometimes we'd go down University and then up to El Cajon Blvd., and then on to Fosters Freeze for fuel. Other times, like today, the mission took us straight down 40th Street to Highway 8. Nevertheless, no matter what course we set out on, we always had orders to look for the big Japanese battleship, the *Goochie-Moochie.*

"Captain, stand by to change speed and to set course to the 70th Street exit."

"Aye, Admiral," I responded with eagerness sitting on my dad's lap, my eight-year-old hands grasping the helm. Next, I slid my right hand down, grasped the column shift lever, and waited impatiently for my next order.

"Standing by, Admiral" I blurted. But to my astonishment, there was no response. I held my position and guided our USS 57 class destroyer down the middle of the right lane at a slight ten-degree angle. We were fast approaching the escape route, and I knew our speed was too fast. We had to change to "all ahead slowly."

"Awaiting orders, sir," I piped out loud.

Then suddenly, Pop shouted, "There it is! The *Goochie-Moochie*! Stand by..."

"But Admiral, we're going to miss the escape route." "Fire all torpedoes!"

Whoosh! I pushed the torpedo knob and got three off. But we were fast approaching the point of no return, and I knew it was now or never. "Torpedoes off sir...standing by for right full rudder and dead slow, sir."

"Very well...stand by for...."

But before the admiral could give me the order, I threw the old column down to the number one position, back and down, and...

The USS 57 let out a tremendous grinding and scraping noise accompanied by a horrendous shudder. We lurched forward then sideways and then forward again. Then two loud explosions rocked us again fore and aft. Suddenly, we could hear the sound of a scraping noise coming from the ocean floor. Clang! Bang! Crash! And finally, thick, black puffs of black smoke bellowed from our engine room.

With a straight face and devotion to duty, the admiral exclaimed, "We've been hit! The *Goochie-Moochie* got us first. Damn! We've been hit! Damage control report!"

"Admiral, we've lost the main engine and drive shaft, sir. We are DIW!"

"Abandon ship! Abandon ship! We're sinking fast. Send the SOS and abandon ship!"

"Aye, sir."

And with these final commands, the USS 57 came to a halt about a hundred yards shy of the 70th Street off-ramp. We jumped ship and swam ashore. We looked back and saw the old 57 dead in the water. Behind her, scattered all over the ocean were rings, nuts, bolts, a gear shaft, and thick black oil.

Within about ten minutes the Coast Guard arrived. "What happened, guys?" the officer inquired.

The admiral snapped to attention (I followed suit) and responded with the uttermost military courtesy. "The Japanese hit us hard, sir. We put up a good fight, but the Goochie-Moochie got us, sir."

Without delay I added, "We were about to maneuver, but her sixteen-inch guns did us in, sir. But I forgot to wait for my dad, uh the admiral, to put in the clutch.

The officer looked my dad square in the eye and said, "Welcome aboard, Admiral. We'll take you to Fleet Headquarters."

The Coast Guard, having recognized my father and being the officer and gentleman that he was, piped us aboard the Coast Guard rescue craft. We set out down Lake Murray Blvd. Soon we turned onto El Paso Street and then made a left onto Avenorra Dr. Nine berths down and we were at Port Dixon.

As we disembarked, the admiral turned to the Coast Guard officer and asked, "Can you escort the captain and me to headquarters please?"

"Why is that, sir?"

"Well, the Chief of Naval Operations is going to feed us beans and gravy for the next ten years. We won't get any liberty for the rest of our lives."

But the good old Mom just shook her head and told us to get ready for dinner.

And the USS 57? Well, they towed her back to port, she underwent repairs, then rejoined the fleet again three weeks later.

Anchors Away!

Dec '95

I sat on my dad's lap, steered the truck, and played "war", while my dad drank beer and remembered the WAR.

Most Valuable Player

It didn't occur to me when I walked onto East High's baseball field that my desire to get involved with baseball would happen so fast. You see, I had given up on a baseball career some fifteen years earlier to become a jockey. Oh, I had made it as a jock, yet I always knew that I had done something my heart was never in. So, after several near-fatal accidents, and a body ravaged by hunger, diet, and drugs, I hung up a million-dollar career and returned home to pick up where I had left off.

I was just walking around in left field, recalling a catch I had made at second base in a colt league all-star game in 1972. We were up by a run and it was the bottom of the seventh and two out. The tying run was at third and the winning run at second. This big redheaded left-handed batter had a count of 3-0 on him. Nobody figured he'd swing with two outs, but he did. I dove to my right, behind second, my body stretched out, eyes closed and gloves opened. The next thing I knew people were cheering, my teammates had gathered around and the game was over. We were champs!

Well, at 5'1", I knew that was the closest I was ever going to get to Yankee Stadium. The rest is history. Until…

* * *

"Hey, man! Get the hell off the field! I gotta water now! We got tryouts today."

I doffed my cap at the old fellow who was yelling at me and proceeded toward the third base line and to the dugout. When I reached the dugout steps, a wrinkled, yet familiar face approached me and blurted out, "I'm sorry, Steve. I didn't know it was you!"

"That's okay, Mr. Bennet," I said, smiling back at the man we used to laugh and joke around with during our high-school days. Frank Bennet had been the head groundskeeper at East High for twenty years. He was a tall, country gentleman who was revered and respected by all. He was my friend through some trying times, and I owed him a lot for the way he used to praise me not for my ball playing, but for my effort.

"Where've you been, Steve? The whole town knows you're back. They say you got in a bad spill and hurt your back and had to quit riding the ponies. Is that true? Wow! You sure were a hero to a lot of kids. You and Bill Walton, are out of the same school! One seven feet, the other five"

"Well, the truth is Mr. Bennet, my heart wasn't in it. It's a different world. I just couldn't adjust to the way of life at the track. Besides, I really missed baseball. I wish there was some way to go back, to be a player, maybe coach someday."

Mr. Bennet apologized to me and then became very serious. "There is, Steve. There's a fifteen-year-old boy who's tried out for this team for two years and hasn't made it. He's a great kid, loves baseball, and like you, wants to be in the Big Leagues. He's always talking about playing for the Yankees. Sound familiar? The only trouble is, the coach won't take a chance on him because he's not a very good hitter. But if you ask me, it's because the boy has been sick and I don't think the school wants to assume the liability for some accident. The boy's name is Tony LaRucca. He's polite and very disciplined. He's a TEAM player, always doing the little things. Like running full speed on easy out ground balls, moving the runners into scoring position, warming up the pitcher, studying the opposition's signs, and coaching first base. He needs some help, Steve. Maybe you'll be the one to help him learn to hit and somehow find a way to get him on the team this year—his senior year! After all, he's not expected to live out the summer."

"Sure, Mr. Bennet. How do I get in touch with him?"

"Well, they're having tryouts at 3:00 p.m. today. Tony is always the first one here, running in centerfield --where he'd love to play someday."

"Thanks, Mr. Bennet. I'll see ya at 3."

That afternoon, under a partially cloudy February sky, I found myself sitting in the bleachers and looking on as some forty young men took ground balls, flies, batting practice, and ran endless wind sprints.

My eyes settled on a frail young man in centerfield, shagging fly after fly, sprinting to wherever the ball was hit with the enthusiasm of a big league prospect at spring training.

After what seemed an eternity, the exhausted youngster jogged off the field and headed for the batting cage. Tony LaRucca came from a poor Italian family on the south side of town. His dad was a grocer and his mom a seamstress. Tony was their only child, and they only wanted the best for Tony. They did everything they could to ensure he got the best education and saw to it that he received every opportunity to succeed. However, a year ago Tony began to miss a lot of school, his grades dropped and he could hardly walk the block to the bus stop without getting out of breath and becoming sick to his stomach. Not long after Tony began to feel this way, his parents took him in for tests. Recently, he was diagnosed as having leukemia. His only goal in life, that of playing for the New York Yankees and winning the MVP as a rookie, was virtually shattered. So Tony set his sights on just one last thing: to make the high-school baseball team, to be a part of, to contribute, to fulfill what was up until now, an impossible destiny.

Every other boy got twenty chances to successfully bunt, hit and run, produce sacrifice flies, and hit away. Nevertheless, when

Tony had had only ten cuts at some very bad pitches, the head coach buried Tony's information card at the bottom of the stack and yelled, "Next guy!"

It was an all-too-familiar scene for Tony, who obediently put his bat back in the rack, grabbed his glove, and sprinted into centerfield.

The agony and frustration showed on Tony's face. His body was drenched in sweat, and he was red-faced and gasping for extra air. But this didn't stop Tony! He set aside the thoughts of the endless injections, weekly chemotherapy, and the inevitable, horrible thought of...death!

With this, I made my way down to the field and walked up to the five-foot-eight-inch lad and introduced myself, "Hi ya, kid. Got a minute?"

The head coach didn't seem to notice, nonetheless care, so Tony and I sat at the end of the first base dugout and got to know each other.

"I've heard of you! You're Steve Morrow, the jockey. You were a celebrity around here along with Bill Walton, the basketball player. They say you played a mean second base on this field and even won an all-star game with a game-saving catch. How come you're back?"

"Well, Tony, I'm not riding horses anymore. I want to be a coach now, and I think we can help each other. You want to make the team and I want to be a coach. You help me and I'll help you. What do you think of that?"

"I'd give anything to make this club, Mr..... uh COACH Morrow! But I can't hit it."

"You listen to me, Tony, and you'll make this team—I promise you!"

I found myself staring dumbfounded into a seventeen-year-olds eyes, trying to hold back the tears. But Tony saw right through me. "Coach," Tony began, "I've got to make this team. I need to learn to hit a curve and then..." He rambled on and on until Tony began to cry. "Can we start today?" "Sure, Tony. I'll go home and get my gear."

I asked the coach and the principal for a week to work with Tony and to see if they couldn't open their hearts. They were unwilling at first but finally agreed that they would give Tony an extra week of tryouts, but that he'd still have to make the team based on his ability and not on his illness. I agreed, and for the next few days, Tony spent three hours a day hitting curveballs. He learned to go with the pitch and became so skilled he began to call out the spots where he was going to hit the ball!

When Tony came to bat the next week, the coach and the players were stunned. The team gathered around and gave him a round of applause. The head coach brought out a box and gave Tony his uniform. The season was to open tomorrow.

Tony turned to everyone and said thank you. He began to speak slowly. "I know that all of you are great ballplayers and being on this team means everything to me. I want all of you to know how lucky you are. You are my friends and I don't ever want you to stop trying, to take what you're doing for granted. Thanks, guys, for showing me what I needed to do to make this team."

Everyone nodded. Then, the coach broke the silence, "Get the gear up and run your laps, guys. Be here at 2:00 p.m. tomorrow and ready to go."

* * *

Into the third week of the season, Tony was hitting .459 and playing a spectacular centerfield. I'd go to all the games, sit in the dugout, and watch as Tony performed like a champion both in the field and at the plate. My heart was filled with joy and I cried every time I looked at Tony grimace with pain after a throw, a swing, or a sprint down the first base line.

It was Thursday, March 11, 1980. East High was scheduled to play Marron, their greatest rival. However, at 9:00 a.m. the phone rang. I was told the game was postponed and that I needed to go to nearby Prescott Hospital ASAP. When I arrived, the entire team was gathered around Tony. Baseballs, bats, and pictures of the New York Yankees lay at the foot of Tony's bed. As I approached, Tony's eyes opened slowly. I leaned forward and Tony asked in a weak voice, "Coach, I won't be playing for the New York Yankees will I?"

"Sure, Tony, you're going to play right beside Babe Ruth and Mickey Mantle."

"And the MVP award?" Tony asked as his eyes opened and closed slowly.

"Tony, you won that award a long time ago."

Tony took one last look at his teammates, tightly gripped my hand, smiled, then closed his eyes for a final time. Tony LaRucca, MVP—MOST VALUABLE PLAYER

In memory of Travis who wanted to be like Tony Gwynn

Three Points of View– Notes on Money

Now, I do not in the least profess to be an expert on economical, political, or theological matters, but I do have practical experience regarding the theme of H A P P O L O G Y, a rare and forgotten topic I shall now attest to my knowledge and share with my brilliant and inquisitive reader a very sad and yet very educational adventure.

After working physically for quite some time in order to pay my bills, I finally had the opportunity to work "mentally" and quickly snatched the rare chance. While doing both, I realized that after riding a racehorse in a race, digging a ditch, carrying some wood, nailing a few braces, and mucking a few stalls, one should receive a greater monetary reward than if one should simply go to school, become a teller of a bank, and at some point, its branch's president. Why? Because, man, the latter only satisfies the greedy side of mankind, while the former is grateful personally for what he actually gets in return. Sweating and becoming sore restores the body's faith in itself while becoming fat, selfish, and smart takes away literally what this life is all about—peace of mind!

However, what of the individual who at one time mucked stalls, washed cars, dug ditches, and shined shoes, then subsequently became fat, smart, and lazy? This then, is not so bad as long as this human being doesn't lose sight of his responsibility toward his family, his God, and to mankind itself.

THINK ABOUT IT!!!
(Christmas 1975; cold, In tack room, no food)

ONE MOMENT PLEASE

The secret to this difficult life is in my heart and my soul, not my wallet and my money. I don't know exactly if it is this nation and what impact it has had on itself, or if it is me and the way other nations have had an impact on me. All I know is that this land of ours is absolutely mad—"double your money," "buy a bigger house," "get a newer car," "take out a bigger loan." What happened to "That's a beautiful flower," "A breathtaking sunset," or "This is a wonderful book"?

Why are our people constantly being brainwashed with money? Throw it AWAY!

I admit, it is impossible (even though I am not a fool!) to get along entirely without it. Nevertheless, hasn't the exorbitant of the whole thing gone on long enough? I mean, what are we? I'll tell you.

We are flesh and blood, body and spirit. What is more, we are nothing more than an urn of ashes, waiting to be scattered at sea. Let us not forget that the spirit itself must attest for us alone someday. This is what we are and it should not be tampered with.

Put your dollar back in your wallet, close it, and open up your heart and soul.

FEB '78 (arrival in Somalia's poverty)

FROM THE GREAT RED BEAR TO THE GREAT WHITE EAGLE

Dear Great White Eagle,

Enough! I am grieved and indignant. We are the mightiest entities on this earth. Come forth, let us roam this earth together in peace, not in hostility.

Thus far, we have each sought ways to destroy mankind. You, by materialism, me by propaganda. I prowl this vast planet for victims, while you hover over the earth seeking your prey.

Wretched are we both!

We preach power, money, fame, and love; yet we both lure and kill in the end. The irony of it all is that one creates the family while the other destroys it. Yet, we all perish in the end. All of us! Whether it be by bullet, car, or disease, we all leave this place, this wonderful earth we so fear to lose.

Come together. And instead of hunting to kill, let us gather our brethren and teach only good to all, not evil.

Your friend,
THE GREAT RED BEAR
MAY '78 (encounter with a Mig 25 over the Med Sea)

Petrushka

"Grandpa Nickolay, my little sister, Milaya, is so cute. And she is so strong. Papa says she looks and acts like Grandmother Petrushka. Does she, Grandpa? Papa says she could be a championline Nana Petrushka. Could she? Tell me about Nana. Papa said you saved her life. He said you protected her and that bad and terrible things happened, but in the end, you were together and you both had a wonderful life together. Please, Grandpa!"

"Slow down, my little star. True, your papa is right. Nana was…well, she was the best. And, yes, it was so hard for her…it was so, so long ago. I was only three, maybe four. Why, I'm old now, twenty-six. It's been so many years. But I remember your beautiful grandmother as if it were only yesterday. Let's see…

"…It was before she won the Village Handicap, the most prestigious race. It began so suddenly and ended so shortly thereafter. My Petrushka! My pride, my joy! How I will always cherish and love her! I miss her so much! She…"

* * *

"Here they come, Nickolay! Paw! Stomp your feet! Try to bite the groom when he puts his hand inside the stall to pour your grain into the feed tub! Get him, Nickolay! Get him! Get him!"

"Hey, you *durok!* You ASS! Get back! Get back, you...you son of a...I'll break your teeth. Try to bite the hand that feeds you! Take that!"

And with those words Sasha, the groom hit Nickolay as hard as he could with his fist, right between the ears. Nickolay scampered to the back of his stall, stood motionless, and stared at Sasha in horror.

The other horses whinnied and neighed, shouting, "Nickolay! Kill him! He's no good! Sasha hurts all of us! Kick him!" As Sasha moved down the shed row, he banged on each door and sent terrified horses running to the back of their stalls too scared to approach their feed bins. Nickolay finally felt him pass for good and hastily but carefully went up to his grain bucket and began to devour the cooked soybeans, whole oats, carrots, and wheat bran that had been mixed with warm water and topped off with molasses and sugar.

After the afternoon graining, all the racehorses in the barn began their usual circling and weaving in their stalls and cribbing on the boards that separated them from each other. They teased each other by doing this, making funny noises and pawing at the walls. Except today, their innocent mischief would be interrupted by a terrible turn of events.

One by one they each stuck their heads out through the webbings of their stall door openings, staring out across the shed row, past the hot-walker area, and to the barn just adjacent to theirs. There you could hear the high whinnying screams of a young horse, a new two-year-old in training.

There, our pock-marked, disheveled, unworthy soul Sasha pulled on the lead rope of a beautiful bay filly named Petrushka. She was a new arrival and came from good bloodlines. She was gentle and willing, but with Sasha, it was a matter of terror for her when she made the simplest of mistakes. On this given day, she had gone the wrong way in the round corral with the trainer. Sasha was upset that she had made him *look bad in front of the trainer.*

Sasha led the poor trembling filly into an abandoned stall. As he pulled her in, she reared her head and screamed for help. Her eyes were wide open and searching for help. She was covered in sweat. She feared for her life. Sasha closed the wooden stall door behind them. Silence fell for a few seconds, then...

"You bitch!" he began, as he lashed the poor thing with a buggy whip on the face, cutting the skin on her nose. Next, he hit her on the flanks, making welts the size of quarters. She quivered at every blow. She reared in defense and Sasha got behind her and flipped her backward. She fell hard to the ground, helpless and in pain.

"Get up, you nickel-bred bitch! I'll teach you to make me look bad! I taught you to lead the right way! You will pay. You will be lucky if you make it out of here."

Sasha punched and kicked her while she was down. He worked himself into a frenzy until he couldn't control himself. He reached into his pocket and pulled out a piece of pipe he always carried, just in case, as he would tell people. He went to grab it but instead kept hitting the Petrushka with the buggy whip.

Petrushka screamed uncontrollably, begging for help. The horrendous cries of all the horses, wanting to help but only able to listen and watch, echoed throughout the entire back side of the racetrack. Nobody came to help her. In Nickolay's barn, all the other horses could do was weave back and forth, rear up, run in circles, run to their doors, stick out their heads and scream in desperation. They could do nothing except stare helplessly at stall number twelve across the way and wait to see if the filly would come out alive.

The noise was horrendous! You could hear the cracking of the whip on the poor, defenseless filly's tender body, followed by the banging of her hooves on the walls. With each blow came yet another shrieking plea for help that carried throughout the barns.

"For God's sake, Nickolay! Help her! Do something! He will kill her for sure! That Sasha is no good. He's buried three of us already. They don't care. The insurance buys two for one of us. Please, Nickolay! You are the biggest and the strongest. He's scared of you the most. Please! Quick!"

The massive seventeen hands, four-year-old colt, paced back and forth. His jet-black, athletic body tensed up as if he was readying himself for a race. His huge frame began to sweat as he paced faster and faster in his stall. He became more and more agitated and angry with each lashing of the whip and Petrushka's screams.

Nickolay had always had feelings for the silky-skinned bay filly Petrushka. He had a crush on her the second she arrived and was led out of the trailer and paraded in front of him on the way to her stall. He was in love with her from the moment he laid eyes on her. At night, they whinnied and nickered and got to know each other. Soon, they were walking on the hot-walker together and playing around. They grew close to each other. Nickolay was always so proud as he galloped around the track and did his workouts. Petrushka would look out of her stall and dream of running with Nickolay someday. At night, they would stare down the shed row at each other and whinny, assuring each other of their affection and protection for each other.

"Nickolay! It is your duty as our leader! And Petrushka is your love. Save her, Nickolay!"

He couldn't take it anymore. Nickolay made a final circle in his ten-by-twelve box stall. He stopped in front of his waterer, reared up, and brought his hooves crashing down on the waterer and the pipe connecting it, smashing it to bits, and sending streams of water shooting in all directions. He backed up against the back wall and with both of his powerful legs, started to kick it with all his might, breaking solid oak panels. He flinched in pain but went on and on, and with every kick a thunderous and deafening BOOM that could be heard throughout the valley.

Whinnying at the top of his lungs, he could be heard all over. He ran up to his door, reared, and struck it over and over again with his shins, putting deep gashes in his legs and bruising his knees. Blood poured out and ran down his fetlocks and hooves. Finally, the door hinges came loose and the door flew open. And none too soon, either.

Petrushka was motionless and barely breathing. Sasha was standing over her with the lead pipe in hand, threatening her and swearing at her. He was ready to deliver the final blow.

Nickolay bolted from his stall, and made a dash across the shed row, past the hot walkers and to the stall where Petrushka was. He wheeled and with all his weight he sent his entire hindquarters and powerful legs into the door. You could hear an explosion as the door burst open. The colt's legs crumpled from the pain. He could hear the horses in his barn yelling, "Kill him! Kill him!"

Sasha's face was ashen, cold. His eyes went blank. He couldn't react. He knew he had gone too far. He managed to grab the buggy whip and get off a quick blow to the colt's face. But there was nothing more he could do to protect himself. Sasha saw a flash of the colt's hind hooves coming at his chest. The blow threw him against the stall wall. He fell in a heap. He managed to stagger to his feet. As he did, he produced the piece of pipe and raised his arm, ready to strike. Another flash, a blur…it was over. Nickolay had let loose the final blow to Sasha's temple. Silence. It was over.

Nickolay went over to Petrushka, bent down, and whinnied to her. She softly looked at him and nickered back. Just then, grooms came running in. It was clear what had happened and they led the colt back to his stall. The vet arrived and cared for Petrushka for a week until she was well enough to walk.

The coroner arrived and took Sasha's body away. Talk circulated throughout the racetrack. Everyone knew how evil Sasha had been and most were glad he had been meted out his payback.

Nickolay could hardly move. He had major injuries to his shins, hooves, and stifles. He would never be the same. A once champion racehorse, he was finished, pressed into service as an outriding horse, and when he became too lame to do this it was decided, because of his bloodlines, that he be put out to stud.

Petrushka went on to win eight of ten stakes races, two handicaps, and the Village Stakes. She truly became the greatest racing mare ever.

On a clear, crisp, sunny November morning, a van pulled up to the Chris Mar Breeding Farm. Nickolay stood at the top of the hill and as soon as he heard the van pull up he ran down to the fence to get a closer look. Then he heard the soft, sweet, familiar nickering of his beloved Petrushka. It was her. He answered back and the neighing became louder and louder. The groom led Petrushka to the gate, opened it, and let her in. As he did, he whispered into Petrushka's ear, "There you go, baby. There is your love. Go to him. Be at peace now."

Petrushka perked up and ran to Nickolay. Together they galloped to the top of the hill. Once there Nickolay cradled Petrushka with his massive body, protecting her - forever. They walked over the hill into the morning sunrise.

* * *

"We had a wonderful life together, your grandmother and I. One day, when I was twenty, I woke up and walked down the hill to the pond where we would meet in the morning to drink and visit. She always got up early and waited there for me. On this particular morning she was lying on her side, a smile on her face, eyes closed in peace. My Petrushka was gone.

"Yes, my dear, your little sister Milaya does remind me of my beloved Petrushka."

Learn 'Em Right

Four young boys, ages six to ten, romp in an open green field. Each joins in a friendly game of tag, howling at one another, kicking their legs high in the air, and flinging their heads back and forth. Twisted strands of brown, black, and blond hair swirl about in the gentle breeze and fall gently over tiny baby faces.

At times, all of them huddle in the middle of the field, their heads barely visible over the tall, swaying blades of orchard grass. There, discussing some matter of extreme significance to them, you can sense the mounting tensions from all the way across the pasture, as the boys begin to argue, point fingers, and chase each other.

It is intriguing to watch the boys. One can sit for hours and never get bored trying to determine if they were playing all, or just some of the time.

Community Hills Development Center is a private school for boys located fifty miles north of San Diego, California. It's tucked away in a beautiful, serene valley between Fallbrook and Highway 395. It encompasses two hundred acres of lush, grassy meadows, an enticing crystal-clear lake, and rolling hills covered in sagebrush and oak trees.

The San Luis Rey River winds its way to the Pacific Ocean passing horse ranches, dairies, and custom ranch-style homes that dot the countryside and mountain peaks overlooking the river valley.

The school itself consists of dormitories for over five hundred students, two athletic fields, several learning centers, a swimming pool, and a dining facility. The staff is made up of a principal, two vice principals, three advisors, forty faculty members, and some thirty aides. Also, located on site is a maintenance department, a bank, laundry, and medical facilities. On the outskirts of the school, near Highway 395, is a grocery store and gas station. The total cost of tuition including room and board is about $900 to $1000 per month.

Community Hills, for over thirty years, has turned out nothing but proven champions. Students come from all over and from all types of backgrounds. Once they arrive, they are given a battery of assessments to see what their potential goals will be, then prescribed their own individual program, and finally assigned a team, which is made up of a lead teacher, assistant teacher, and several aides.

"Hey, Howie. How many ya got this year?"

"Thirty, Corey. From the third grade to the fifth."

"Man, I've got about twenty-five, but there's this one kid who is a real case. They've kept him back for the last couple of years."

"What's his problem?"

"Can't get along with the others most of the time. Hardly ever works. A real screw-up. Gets on my nerves almost every day. Loves the attention, but always the wrong kind."

"Look, Corey. I've been meaning to talk to you. I know which kid you are speaking of, and I don't think he's as bad as you say."

"What do you mean?"

"Well, remember the kid you had a couple of years ago, a seven-year-old named Ronnie? Remember how you worked with him on the side? You took him for walks down the road, took him to the beach, to the mountains. You only took him to the track a couple of days a week. Three months later you entered him in the

Youth Race and he came in second. From then on it was a breeze with him. And you always kept your promise and took him for his walks, talking to him about his family and what other things he liked to do. He had confidence in you. He grew up to be an Olympic athlete and had a family of runners himself."

"Oh, how can I forget," said Corey. "Took me the longest time to get his trust. But you're right; it worked. And I coached his eldest son who was great right out of the gate."

"Corey, ATTITUDE! Your attitude toward this new kid, what's his name, Jason? Well, it's too negative. You need to be more positive, quit doing the "norm," and find new tricks. So, when he's making a fuss, kicking, and biting, you can distract him by using new techniques that will keep him focused on what he has to do, even if it's a reward of some kind, which I know YOU don't like to give."

Jason Baxter, alias JB as he was known. Stood well over six feet and weighed a ton for his age. With fire in his coal black eyes, his huge misshapen nose always turned up in the air, and his swaying gait, all gave the impression that there was always only one thing on JB's mind—trouble. Why?

Jason's father had been a professional athlete. He was one of the best sprinters in the world. And in the hurdles, he was second to none. His father had gone on to be a successful breeder of racehorses. His mother was a prominent dancer and star in her own right. Having tried track, she switched to dancing on a square stage on the weekends, prancing from side to side and high-kneeling with the best of them.

Jason was an only child raised in the country and had little to do but run all day in the fields and raise havoc with the animals that were on the farm. At night, he lay in his room, thinking about the world that he would soon see and all the attention he would soon be getting.

When he got older, some of the boys from the other farms would be brought over and allowed to play with Jason. He quickly became jealous and became a bully. From the moment he entered school, he was never free from trouble, always picking on some other kid or getting into some mischievous situation where he would end up breaking things.

Eventually, Corey became his teacher and each time Corey began to explain a lesson, Jason would gaze out across the wide open terrain, his thoughts galloping aimlessly, hopping from hillock to hillock. He'd have fantasies of himself leaping valleys and finally roaming off into the distance, head held high and prancing over the horizon. At other times when Corey would be walking alongside, Jason would suddenly scream out, bolt to the side, kick something, and run away. It was a constant struggle. He was surely defiant and this was going nowhere positive.

But the worst behavior occurred in a PE class one day when the students went to the track at 9:00 a.m. to run a mile. Once there, Jason argued, fought, and disrupted the entire class so badly that Corey had to personally walk him the opposite way of all the others and then turn him around and jog with him—two miles!

Corey made a recommendation for an IEP (Individualized Education Plan) and a meeting was arranged between Jason, Corey, and his aides. The plan called for Jason to go to PE with Corey alone early in the morning before school started and then gradually be allowed to integrate back in with the other students.

The new program started on a Monday. Skip gave Corey some more much-needed advice: "You need to earn his respect before he gives you any."

At 5:00 a.m. the crimson sun had barely risen above Los Coches peak. The gentle cooing of the morning doves had begun to arouse the farmers, signaling another work-filled day. Work crews clambered down from their bunks, donned blue-denim overalls and cowboy boots, then scampered off across the open track and to their respective duties.

Corey reached into his Levi's jacket pocket and fumbled around for the master key. He clasped it, slowly took it out, then quietly slipped it into the keyhole. He turned the key as quietly as possible counter-clockwise until he heard the familiar "click." He paused and started inside. Jason had been asleep and upon hearing the click raised his head to see who had entered his room. All six feet of him sprang up out of his bed. He became agitated and restless, as this was NOT his normal routine.

"Jason," Corey began, "time to go. We're going to the track early today, before all the other boys. Come on, kid. Let's go. You can do it."

Corey backed up a few paces as Jason came closer, sighed, and rubbed his eyes. Without a word he stared at Corey, undecided or just too sleepy to respond. He stretched, bent his legs, and arched his neck. He sighed again. He looked more confused than ever and started to shake a little. To Corey, he seemed somewhat rebellious, but nevertheless, offered no resistance. In fact, he kind of liked the personal attention, something he craved.

"Come on, Jason. PE starts now. You will like it. Just you and me."

Corey led Jason down the wide hall, out the wooden door, and onto the dirt path that led to the track. As soon as both of them turned toward the track, Jason started to act up. He flailed his arms in the air as if swatting at flies, and he struck out behind him with his right leg, crushing the knee of his imaginary assailant. He screamed at the top of his lungs, pleading for all the other boys to come to his rescue or just pay attention to him. It worked because some of the boys woke up and stuck their heads out the windows to see what was happening. "Look, it's Jason, everyone!" They urged him on, "Go Jason go!" Corey did all he could to fight back his own anger and frustration. He held Jason's hand tight and kept walking, never looking Jason in the eyes, but in a reassuring voice kept repeating, "It's okay, you're okay."

As they approached the track, Jason calmed down slightly. He looked out upon the track and noticed nobody was on the track except him and Corey. Corey asked Jason in a firm voice, "Now,

Jason, I want you to run a mile on your own. It will be good for you. Stay on the rail and try to concentrate on your breathing and your stride." Corey no sooner got the words out of his mouth than Jason had disappeared at full speed into the predawn mist that enveloped the track.

He went berserk, running as fast as he could on the inside part of the track. Halfway around he stopped, turned around, and chased a loan coyote who had made his way down an embankment on the track. Realizing that he couldn't match the coyote's speed, Jason gave up, turned around again, and jogged slowly on the outside portion of the track near the rail. He looked beyond the administration building, over the glen, and across the river. He saw the silhouettes of two yearlings standing on a hillock that overlooked the facility. They were staring dumbfounded at Jason while he ran, kicked at rocks, threw sand, and shouted funny and strange noises at them.

After what seemed to be an hour, but was only five or six short minutes, Jason made his way back to the main gap where Corey had been patiently waiting for him. Jason jogged up to Corey, glanced at him, lowered his quivering head, and shuffled three or four steps sideways. There he stood, motionless, as if anticipating Corey's next command. But Corey merely said, "Looks like you had fun," and then he turned and walked away.

In the beginning, Jason felt relieved to be away from the other children. But then as the days went by he began to actually miss the company of the others. He started to realize why everyone hated him and why he lashed out at them; he always sought the *wrong* kind of attention. He understood now by behaving and being nice, he would fit in. He wanted to be like the others and to belong, and he understood that being a bully and being defiant wasn't going to get him anywhere in life. It would only make him more miserable in the end. He was going to try.

As time progressed, Jason developed a strong sense of self-accomplishment. He would set a small goal for himself, running a half mile at a steady pace, concentrating on his breathing, and shutting out any distractions. The magpies went unnoticed, the coyotes kept clear of the track, and the yearlings looked on with pride.

Jason was soon running a smooth, quick mile, while Corey stood at the rail with a stopwatch in his hand and a lump in his throat.

Jason's schoolwork began to improve as well. His relationships with his peers and his teachers began to get better each day. He became likeable and was sometimes sought out by his classmates for advice or assistance. Through praise and patience, dedication, and determination, Jason was soon becoming a leader.

In the course of three months, Jason gradually worked himself back into the regular PE class. Little by little he came out later and later in the morning, amid more and more company.

Instead of being the belligerent punk whom everyone despised, he became the champion whom everyone admired.

* * *

One cold February morning, Skip approached Corey while Jason was doing his workouts and inquired, "Hey, big race next month. Think he's ready?"

Corey had a big grin on his face, "Yep, physically and mentally. Doing good at school and in the dorm too."

"Well Corey, it may be just the thing. A mile race. He'll probably do well. Nobody around these parts runs the mile any faster these days. Hey, it will be his graduation present and reward."

"Thanks, Skip. I'll enter him tomorrow."

* * *

March 5, 1975

The announcer's voice crescendos:

"...and they're turning for home with a quarter of a mile left to go. It's Jason Baxter moving up strong in the middle of the track.... It's JB, Ladies and Gentlemen, taking the lead with Royal Azure second and Attack third...it's Jason Baxter...JB opening by three lengths! And JB wins the Del Mar Stakes. What a finish folks!"

"Well, Corey. Looks like he's gonna be okay."

"Yeah, Skip. Thanks for all your help."

"Well, you know yourself; sometimes it can be awfully tough trying to grow up."

Jason Baxter went on to win his next six races plus the Million Dollar Badger Handicap. He retired at the age of seven and lived out his life at San Luis Rey Downs in his beloved pastures where he played as a little boy. He lived to the ripe old age of twenty-two.

That's what you get when you,

LEARN 'EM RIGHT

A Moment of Despair

"Now, Yuri, why are you sitting by the stove, all hunched up like a lump of coal? And why that distant look through bleak and glassed eyes? What is it this time, lad? Has Vilna, your little mongrel dog, gone off with that little terrier mutt again? Or did Papa take all your allowance away again to pay for his vodka?

"Why, Yuri? Why are you so gloomy, full of doom? You're sitting, warming your pathetic body by the stove whilst your heart grows colder by the second. Come, Yuri, tell Tetya, your dear old uncle, your misfortunes. I mean, as God is my witness I have seen an abundance of trials and tribulations in my sixty-one years; some almost killed me, others came close. Out with it, Yuri!"

But Yuri sat, stoned face, knees to his chin, leaning against the stove. His hands were folded and clasped around his knees. He stared down into the flame that burned inside the old coal stove. He was listening but heard very little. He just couldn't help it. Why, he knew exactly what was wrong. He could recite the same words over and over again.

"SHTO DELAT?" ("What to do?")

"Yuri! Get up! Help Dmitri feed the animals! Our neighbors eat corn millet and mush and you are deep in thought over some trifle you don't have in your possession? You're good for nothing lacky! I'll show you in the spring when you pick the harvest! You'll

118

appreciate just being alive when I get through with you! I'll work you like a muzhik I will! You'll see!"

Yuri turned his head away from his uncle's voice and peered out the ice-covered window in the back of him. All he could see was white, cold snow. Cold, like his heart, as his uncle said. It would never be warm again.

"Yuri! Go! Now!"

Yuri suddenly, slowly, forcefully looked over at his dear uncle and smiled, then turned back toward the endless snow. In a calm and monotone voice, he muttered, "My little mongrel Vilna, as you referred to him, was killed by Kalinka's shepherd this morning, dear uncle."

Yuri rose, put on his coat and gloves, and went to help Dmitri feed the animals.

The Promise

"Why my little comrade Misha? I have seen you all morning, doing nothing. You sit perched upon this stone wall contemplating. What is it, my lad? Have the doves abandoned you - again?

I suppose you cleaned all of Mitrofin's muddy paddocks for nothing again. He promises you our own pony, a saddle, and silver spurs. How long will you continue to do his bidding for nothing but the emptiness you feel now?

You walk miles on end doing odd jobs for a few kopecks. You put that raggedy gray shirt on and that black frayed tie, and you knock on every shopkeeper's door and you BEG! 'Please sir, I have experience in all facets of life. May I please sweep, stock your shelves, make tea for your children and cakes for your Mrs? I am educated. I can teach the languages to your sons and...', and on and on your walk. Each proprietor promises you a ruble here and there if you will only come back tomorrow.

My God lad! Are you still walking the countess' must for a muffin a week? Are you still listening to your best friend Alyosha tell you that 'Next week we will play Misha'. And when you ask her if she feels the same you always get the same answer, 'Of course I do my little puppy, but I will have to arrange things. Don't worry, I will!' Then, Misha, the very next second she is saying something indignant, but oh, it's your desperate mind that is warped, not hers!

My little Misha, why have you lost your way? You had so many good things. Now look at you a measly servant boy! Most young men your age have an izba to live in, a caring wife, a multi-paying ruble job with the government, or a count. They have children that proudly and willingly walk beside them. They are rich and knowledgeable about their ancestors and their sacrifices.

These young men are stable, accountable, and never tolerate bashing of any kind. Their wives admire them without condition.

But you, Mishenka, my scoundrel, you clean the hogs, wash and milk the cows, feed the chickens and then you sit on this rock wall, the boundary of your very soul, and you wonder what is out there that you can be honored for. You look at the distant forest, searching for that person who will immortalize your soul when you have walked up and over the mountain.

MISHA! GET UP YOU LAZY SLOTH AND FEED MY GOATS, GROOM AND SADDLE MY HORSE. AND, IF YOU DON'T HAVE A RETORT TO THIS TONGUE-LASHING, IF YOU CLIP AND BRAID THE MARE'S MANE, POLISH HER HOOVES AND WRAP HER TAIL IN FEATHERS TO SHOW HER TODAY, I WILL TAKE YOU TO THE FAIR NEXT WEEK TO SEE NATASHA AND FELINKOV. NOW, WHAT DO YOU SAY TO THAT, MY LITTLE COMRADE?"

"YOU PROMISE UNCLE!? YOU PROMISE!?"

"OF COURSE I DO MISHA?"

A Member Of
The Rest Of The Fools

«... Tell you, gentlemen, my fine suiters, do you not know what awaits us? Why just the other day it was reported to me that we are receiving wagons of gold and silver that were locked away in a vault in Omsk for years! And, to add to this fortune, every citizen is receiving 500 rubles!"

"And you Sergij. What's in it for you? Tell us YOUR fortuitous situation."

"Why I interviewed with the Count himself! He told me that I am going to be appointed guardian of all the fortune! After all, I worked in a bank for a month! And, I interviewed with the academy and they are giving me the position of Master Finance Lecturer. After all, I did teach mathematics for several years. I have talked to and have met countless prominent leaders and business owners of late, and they have assured me, due to my unique history, that I shall be put in charge of many firms, and many reputable organizations. After all, I have done almost everything and they have all stated that I am more than qualified."

"Well then Sergij, answer us this; why, after months have they not called you to fill these positions? And did you know there are no wagons of gold and silver? And what about teaching at the university? They are closing it next month! There is no funding due to the war. Most students have been sent to the front! Master Finance Lecturer? There never was such a position and there never will be. Tell me Sergij, what did you do to receive all these false promises? What?

Tell us!

You think we are a bunch of old wall hackers who do nothing? We are successful retired gents with meaningful and sustained histories. We have intact, living, caring, and extended families. How in our right minds would we believe the likes of you? Now, take your filthy mut of a pooch, your tiny useless self, and go back to the park where you are a member of the rest of the fools!"

The Mystery of Cowles Mountain

PROLOGUE

The last story is based on true events. It is about a still, ongoing horrific journey in one's life. It is intertwined with local history, family heritage, the spirit world, and much, much more. Some call it science fiction; others call it real life. Notwithstanding, it is an incredible turn of coincidental events that simply evolved over time and led to the most bizarre outcome.

Along the way you will "feel" what is happening. You will feel the Great Spirit, sense the footsteps in the hall, hear the coyotes howl at night, and, if you're lucky, catch a glimpse of the old man running down the hallway at 1:00 a.m. Still, better, to see what's in the bottom of the well...

The Mystery of Cowles Mountain has been told in the classroom for thirty-one years to select audiences.

Ready?

Part I
Annual Visit

Office of Dr. Ruben Garcia II Psychotherapist
Suite 62

I hated coming here. I've been coming here since I was eight. Well, the address has changed. Now, I see Dr. Ruben Garcia II, after having many visits with his deceased father while growing up.

The office is in Normal Heights some two miles from the San Diego Zoo. It sits up the hill from Balboa Park on University Ave. It's just a small, white-washed office with the usual sign on the door. The waiting area has a few chairs, a table with medical journals, and a lamp in the corner; soft music plays continually through a speaker hanging above the entrance to the doctor's office.

"So, Mike, another year has gone by. You're sixty-one now. So, how have you been? Any activity? Any voices? Any footprints? How about the old man? Does he appear at all anymore?"

"Wow, Dr. Garcia! Has it been that long? Your father was so good to me. You have been so good to me. Ah, no. No activity. Not for years now. Except the usually prescribed telling of the story to my students every Halloween. Your dad was right; by sharing the episode, it wards off the spirits from returning."

"Do you ever have visions in your head?"

"I dream sometimes, maybe twice a year. I see his face, feel his beard, smell his breath. He's not holding the knife like he did in the beginning, and instead of hovering over me, leaning over me while I sleep, he's just standing next to my bed. My dog still barks and walks around."

"Anything else?"

"No, my bed still faces the window and the closet door. The closet door is always closed, the chest is locked, and the crow is inside it. I still awake at 1:15 a.m. and check everything. And just as all the other dogs did, Shilo walks the house with me. But he can sense him. He growls sometimes, then whimpers and lies down in front of the closet door.

"But there haven't been any coyotes, no blood stains on the walls, outside or in, no muddy footprints on the carpet in the living room, no open doors, and no cries of 'Help me! Help me, little boy!' The last time I heard those chilling cries was when I was thirty."

"Do you still go to the water tower, Mike?"

"Every year, Doc. The base of the well is covered with dead flowers I've left. I bring fresh ones every year, on October 30. And still, nothing will grow around the tower. More oddly, businesses there continue to come and go with two burning down within the last twenty years.

"Oh, and I still hike the trail up 'S,' I mean Cowles Mountain. I visit the entrance to the burial ground and walk around where the house and barn were, where Don and I found everything that fateful day back in 1962. Other than that, Dr. Garcia, I'm doing great! I got remarried last year. Funny thing. My wife set up the bedroom furniture, and when I came home I had to change it all around. She asked me why and I told her that I'd tell her someday. 'But for now, honey, always keep the closet door closed.' See you next year, Dr. Garcia"

Part II
Why I Am Who I Am

My father, Donald R. Dixon was a former twenty-six-year navy veteran, WWII pilot, and former gas station owner who semi retired at the age of seventy-five, retired at eighty-eight, and passed away peacefully in his sleep at ninety-eight, only four years ago.

He had grown up in Utah, Idaho, and Wyoming. His father was a Dane who became a telegrapher on the railroad.

My grandmother, however, had a different past. Her mother was Cherokee and her father was Danish. But she had, well, two moms. My Danish Mormon great-grandfather had taken Grandma's full-blooded Cherokee mother on the trek with them from North Carolina, along with his first wife, Rebecca. You get the picture.

Grandma Kristie loved to cook Danish food but adored traditional Cherokee teachings, language, rituals, and clothing; she held on to her roots and eagerly passed them on to anyone in the family who would listen—that was, huh, only me.

Dad got sick of the church's teachings, as did Grandmother, and they departed Utah and headed for Riverside, California. There, at sixteen, Dad persuaded Grandma Kristie to lie about his age to join the Navy. That's why, when Dad died we actually found two birth certificates—so he may have been ninety-nine when he died.

How he got to that old age, we don't know. He was a drinker and smoker for fifty-five years, not to mention a ladies' man. So, how my dear little mom stayed married to this man for seventy-three years, God only knows! But she did. And she raised two kids, me and my brother Don, who is nine years older than me.

Mom's parents came from Russia and Poland. Grandma was a beautiful Polish woman whom I never knew, due to the fact she died from tuberculosis right after my mother was born. She was twenty-six. My grandfather was a violinist from Russia, half Cossack horseman, and half Muscovite.

My mom's family was originally Jewish. I say that because one aunt became a Catholic, one uncle a Methodist, and still another uncle a rabbi! My mom said the Lord's Prayer once a day and that was it. She taught me both Christianity and Judaism. And my dad, being an ex-Mormon, well, made it kind of confusing, but I "believed." My brother on the other hand was so confused and became an atheist!

Mom, an inspiring haiku writer, held the family together. Dad was away for much of my brother's upbringing, but he was home when I was growing up, having retired when I was two years old. Aside from his debauchery, Pops always had time to teach us how to hunt and fish, coach our Little League teams, and take us to Padre games at Westgate Park to see my cousin Ken Hunt pitch. Oh sure, he'd stay in the bars till 2:00 or 3:00 a.m. and I'd have to go in and get him to come out, but he always came home, singing and crying to my mom. A few "SOBS" from Mom, three hours of yelling at him, and he was always forgiven—until the next time.

My brother left home when he was eighteen so I was pretty much by myself. I only had a few friends, but we always played sports, went hiking and fishing, and always hung out together.

But my favorite person to be around was my grandmother. She taught me the Cherokee ways, taught me to respect nature and animals, showed me how to appreciate life, and brought into my life, THE GREAT SPIRIT. It was from her that I learned about the "SIXTH SENSE," "SPIRITUAL FEELING," and "SPIRITUAL INTERPRETATION." And it was my grandmother who taught me the history, the true history, about my own people and my own region. And this had everything to do with our story.

Part III
Unknown History

The history books will tell you that San Diego was at one time a whaling city, home of the navy fleet, a fisherman's paradise, and the site of the first Jesuit mission, San Diego de Alcala. They'll tell you that Mexico owned the land after the Spanish, along with the rest of California. After gold was discovered and California subsequently became a state, San Diego became a great hub for trading, transportation, and new businesses. Well, it's all true. But the history books, aside from merely mentioning the small towns in north and east counties and providing a line or two of how they were founded, leave out the most important historical aspect: the

Native Americans of San Diego County. It is only today that we can sadly and regretfully look back and admire what they did here.

My grandmother Kristie knew a lot about East San Diego County, especially Cowles Mountain. She had spent time there as a little girl, not as the granddaughter of a white settler, but the proud little girl of our Native American history. Nana would tell her stories about the Kumeyaay and Cuyamaca Indians who would make their yearly trek from the Cuyamaca Mountains, some fifty miles east of what is now El Cajon. They followed the deer trails down the slopes of the San Diego River banks, which ran past Cowles Mountain and eventually on to the Pacific Ocean.

The San Diego River flowed at the foot of Cowles Mountain. It was here that the Cuyamaca and Kumeyaay would camp, grind their corn, and bury their loved ones in a cave facing the Pacific Ocean. After each ritualistic burial, they would conceal the entrance with large boulders and branches. The cave itself was situated in a partial ravine and thus somewhat naturally hidden and protected.

Grandma's stories filled my heart with excitement and curiosity, much to the point that when we were old enough, my friends and I would roam Cowles Mountain for days on end searching for that cave. Then, finally, in 1965, my friend Bill Taylor, literally "FELL" into it! After sliding down a crevice he ended up standing in the cave surrounded by pottery, bones, arrowheads, and mummies!

We never took anything, and we are sure nobody else did either. Then, in 1967, the tomb was sealed forever by an earthquake. Since then, I've tried to relocate it every so often but to no avail.

Part IV
Irish Immigrants

Calvin and Lucy McGurdy came to San Diego by way of a steamship from Ireland in 1893 with their two children, John and

Sally Mae McGurdy. Calvin took out a claim outside the county in what is now San Carlos, a forty-acre parcel located at the foot of our famous Cowles Mountain and about a hundred yards from the river on the first foothill. Across from where is now Mission Trails Golf Course

Calvin and Lucy raised cattle, goats, and chickens. Both the children helped with the family business and were home-schooled on the Bible, Latin, math, and history. John, the eldest, liked to visit with the local Native Americans and work with the cattle, while Sally Mae became a musician, playing the violin, and serenading the cattle at night. Life was peaceful and routine.

Tragically, at eight, Sally Mae was bitten by a rattlesnake while working around the barn. Efforts by doctors and the local Natives to save her life failed. She was only eight when she died.

Calvin and Lucy, as you could imagine, never recovered. Calvin became an alcoholic and succumbed to the liquor at forty-five. Lucy committed suicide a year later. John was all alone, at fifteen.

John had been doing a good job tending to the ranch, and at twenty met a fine Danish woman named Anna. They married and had three children: John Jr., Gretchen, and Laura.

The ranch prospered with the sale of meat and hides to the settlers and to the railroad. The children went to school, mingled with the local settlers and Native Americans, and lived a life of leisure and fun.

The area was vast and there was plenty to do. People got along and there was always work to be done for a fine profit. San Diego was in its infant stages of growth.

John continued to trade with the Kumeyaay and Cuyamaca. He promised them that he would never sell the mountain land and would always keep it for them to use. That's why to this day Cowles Mountain is still in its natural state, the way it was over a hundred years ago.

Gretchen and Laura left home at eighteen to pursue careers in San Francisco. They returned home only once and after all these years nobody had ever heard from them or their whereabouts.

John Jr. became a local businessman, but he was involved with the wrong crowd, making deals and profiting, all at the hands of some crooked deals. What's worse, he was always borrowing money from his father. And as you can imagine, the cattle business was dying out. So much so that John had to sell his riverfront property to pay debts. All that was left was the house, barn, pens, the well, and the mountain, which he would never part with, keeping his promise to his Cuyamaca and Kumeyaay brothers and sisters.

John lived a solitary life after John Jr. left for the East Coast in 1940. Then in 1947, John himself just disappeared! Vanished! A friend saw his cattle wandering the riverbank and went to check on him. The table had breakfast on it, the house was a mess, chickens were loose, and the goats were roaming about. But, John was missing. People looked everywhere. Searches were conducted. But nothing.

After five years, the county took over the property, sold the livestock, and abandoned the buildings. It was deemed open land to the public to use up to the foothills, but, (as John promised), no structures could be built on the mountain. John's estate went into holding, but there was an entire bank account of some $65,000 in savings missing!

By the 60s, the buildings started to decay pretty badly. The barn had half collapsed, the pens were torn down, and the house's roof had caved in. Vandals had pretty much destroyed or taken everything. But the one thing that stood out, only partially overgrown, was the white quarry rock well that Calvin had dug in 1893. Its white-washed stone still glistened in the sun. And you could still draw water from the well…

Part V
Up The Mountain

It was 1961. I was six. We had moved into my parents' "dream house" at 6080 Avenorra Dr. La Mesa, California. It was a modest three-bedroom, two-bath track home two blocks from Lake Murray and a mile from Cowles Mountain.

There was nothing but open land, a flowing San Diego River at the foot of the mountain, and plenty of fish and game to last for years.

My friends and I always played in the canyons, fished at the lake, and roamed the hills. But our favorite outing took place on the last Saturday of every month when we meticulously planned, gathered our packs and canteens, and headed up the face of "S" Mountain, named at the time for all the SDSU (San Diego State University) students who went up once a year and made an "S" out of painted white rocks on the southwest face.

We trudged through brush, and culverts, and climbed over rocks. There were no marked trails back then. Oh sure, there was the utility road that led to the radio tower at the top, but what fun would that have been?

During winter rains, our favorite thing was to climb up the treacherous "Eastern Rock," as we called it, and sip from "Cowles Falls," as we named it.

At day's end, we clamored down exhausted, went home, showered, and then met at someone's house for a BBQ. If it was during the summer, we'd all pile into the bed of Dad's '57 Ford truck and head out to Westgate Park to see the Padres play and hopefully catch a game when Ken Hunt, our cousin, was pitching.

It was August, hot, 102 degrees. I was sitting on the porch with our dog Ziggy, petting her while I watched my brother wash his '58 Ford. Dad was at the gas station working, and Mom was at the store. When Don was done he looked at me and said, "Go get the keys to the Jeep."

As always, I obeyed. I got them right away and brought them to him. "What?" I asked in my little boy's inquisitive voice, "Where are we going?"

"Get in. We're going up the mountain." "Where?"

"The McGurdy house. Nobody will be there. It's too hot, let's go."

"But it's haunted. We're not allowed to." "We're going. Let's go. Get in."

Off we went. We crossed the river and started up the access road. About a quarter mile from the river and the first hillock, we stopped in front of an old post.

"Donnie, we're not supposed to be here."

"Quiet. I'm going to the barn. You go in the house. Don't be scared. Nobody's here."

As I was heading to the house, I passed the well, a white rock-based circle about six feet round. The bucket still hung on the bar, and it was still drawing water. I hated to go near the well. I always got the chills and while I wanted to look down at it, at the same time I was always so scared. I ran away from it.

I made my way to the front door, which was askew and leaning sideways. I was about to enter when I heard my grandmother's voice, "The spirit doesn't want you here; you're going to be in trouble."

It felt wrong, but I HAD to go in.

My brother slipped into the barn. It was dirty, dusty, and moldy with cobwebs everywhere. The roof was partially caved in on one end, beams had fallen through the ground, and there were remnants of stalls lining the sides of the barn. Horseshoes and nails littered the ground along with old, rotten pieces of leather. There were rusty bridles and bits hanging near the entrance to the barn door, which had holes in it from kids throwing rocks at it. But even in its dilapidated state, it meant something, held meaning, and told a story.

As pigeons flew out from the rafters and scared Don, he continued to the back near the last stall and broken feeders. He took a stick and poked around. He noticed something reflecting off the board behind the feeder and stuck the stick into a small gap. The nail from the feeder popped out, and after a little prying the board came loose. To his astonishment, an old rusted-out small pistol fell to the ground. There were no markings. Don looked around as if to see if anyone was watching. He grabbed the pistol and stuck it in his pocket. He ran as fast as he could outside and began to call me, "Mike! Let's go!"

At six I had no fear, but I did have a lot of curiosity. I felt as if I had entered some magic castle, went back to the "olden days," and simply "discovered" something old.

I walked through the vandalized kitchen, which still had some broken plates on the wooden table, broken bits of cups and saucers on the floor, and cupboards open, bashed in, and their doors ripped off the hinges.

My heart was pounding. I could feel it. I was overcome with a "freezing" sensation as if someone or something was right next to me. Scared to death I made it down the hallway and into the first of two small bedrooms. There was broken glass, old clothes, graffiti on the walls, beer cans, and trash everywhere. Other than that, the room was empty, cleared out by thieves long ago.

I tiptoed out avoiding the shards of glass and went down the hallway further to the last bedroom. Unlike the other bedroom, the door was still affixed. As I pushed it open, I stood for a moment at the entrance and glanced all around. I felt "something." I wanted to run but I went in. It too had broken glass and was covered in graffiti. There was a closet that was open, empty, and littered with rat droppings. The room smelled awful. But unlike the smaller bedroom, there was a box spring frame in the corner underneath the broken window. There were several rolled-up old, muddy carpets underneath. I bent down, forcing myself to ignore the putrid stench, and with a stick I had found lifted up the carpets, one by one. There it was an old, tattered, and worn-out red-and-black plaid long-sleeved Pendleton shirt. Two buttons were missing, there were several rat-eaten holes in one of the sleeves, and on the left side pocket a hole, well, more like a slice at an angle. And all around it a dark, reddish-brown stain. Was it...?

"Mike! Let's go! Someone's coming!"

I froze. But something told me, "Take it." I grabbed the shirt and ran out of the room, back down the hallway, outside, and jumped in the jeep. As we sped off an old green Rambler came around the corner. He didn't see us, hopefully.

"Donnie, what did you find?"

"Something bad! And an old rusty pistol. And before I left the barn I found an old knife with dark stains on the broken blade and on the handle. You?"

"An old shirt with a hole over the heart and a dark stain! What are we going to do with these things?"

"Put 'em in your toy box. Nobody will look there."

Part VI
Help Me, Little Boy! Help Me!

It all began at seven years old, really! That was when things got pretty weird, every night at about 1:00 a.m. I would hear noises in my closet, footsteps in the hallway, backyard, and on the side of the house. And each night, I could hear the whisper of an old man's voice, "Help me, little boy. Help me."

It got so bad that my dog Ziggy would howl, jump on my wall outside my window, and scrape her paws on the side of the house, leaving blood marks. I would run down the hallway and wake my mom and dad up, "Mommy, Daddy, there's a man in the house and outside."

This would only be met with harsh punishment and scolding. I could hear my brother saying, "Go back to sleep, you little baby."

After months of this, it escalated. I could hear my toy box open in my closet and things being taken out. I would get up in the morning, the door would be open, the chest wide open, and all the things we had gathered were on the floor: the knife, the pistol, and the Pendleton shirt.

The old man's voice became louder and his words more profound and threatening. After several months, I would awaken in a sweat, frozen with fear, as I stared at a man leaning over me or standing by my bed each morning at 1:00 a.m., saying over and over, "Help me, help me."

My parents never believed me. I would get blamed for doors open in the morning, muddy footprints on the living room floor, and worst of all, for waking everyone up with crying and screaming.

It got so bad I was taken to a hypnotist and a psychotherapist. Under hypnosis, I told the same story each month for two years! And at each doctor's visit, I drew the same picture of the old man: gray beard, dressed in Levis, and wearing that black-and-red tattered Pendleton shirt with the hole in the chest.

Was it ever going to end? Two more years of suffering, doctors, isolation, and punishment. Then, at ten years old, on one particular night, the old man appeared as usual but only this time he was holding the knife and the gun. Not in a threatening manner, but as if to show me something.

We hadn't been to the McGurdy house in years, but one Saturday we went back. It was worse than ever—almost completely destroyed now. Yet, the well stood tall, somewhat still overgrown with scrub oak. I walked over to it and looked down. I got the chills, started to panic, and ran to the Jeep. Don asked me, "What is it with you and the well?"

"I don't know. But I get really scared when I go near it."

Part VII
Cops Everywhere

I was twelve. Grandma was visiting and we were talking about the crow, the eagle, and the hawk and what they mean to Native Americans. She was teaching me "signs" of animals. Then she asked me, "Have you helped him yet?"

Shocked, I said, "Grandma, NO! You believe me?"

"Yes," she replied. "Of course. You have the sixth sense-spiritual sense. It won't be long; he'll tell you what to do." Sunday, 9:00 a.m. Three La Mesa police cars rolled up with two county sheriff units and a San Diego Police unit. We were all out front. "Is this the Dixon residence?" one of La Mesa's police officers asked.

My dad walked over and answered, "Yes, sir, why?"

The officer looked at my brother and me and asked, "You Don, and Mike?"

"Yes, sir," we replied in unison.

"Sir, can I ask your boys some questions?" "Sure," my dad said.

All the officers were standing around; one was holding a Dictaphone to record our answers.

"We are investigating a cold case, the disappearance of John McGurdy, who hasn't been seen since 1947. We saw your jeep up on the mountain yesterday. We asked around. People say you used to go up the mountain to his ranch a lot. So—"

My dad interrupted, "Officers, plenty of people go up and take things."

"Sir, please. Now, boys, some of your friends at school have told us you took some things, and you've shown them some things, Is that true?"

"Who hasn't?" my brother snapped.

"We just want to know if you've found any weapons or anything like that. Also..." The officer took out a photo. He asked us, "Have you ever seen this man?"

I blurted, "It's him! Only younger. He's wearing the shirt! He has a beard. It's him!"

The officer asked what I meant. In the meantime, my brother stared at me, and Dad said, "Oh my God!"

"Officer wait!" I ran into the house and got the drawings. I showed them to him.

His jaw dropped. Everyone stared at me. Grandma was now on the porch. She was smiling. She whispered audibly, "They promised to watch over him. You'll see."

"What did you boys take?"

I ran into the house and came out with the old pistol and broken knife. Then, when I showed the officers the shirt, I thought they were going to faint. They just became quiet, looked at me, and asked, "You know anything else?"

Then the sheriffs suggested we go up the mountain to the house.

My family got in the jeep, and a caravan of police and sheriff cars headed up to the McGurdy place. When we got there a woman officer came up to me and asked, "Mike, is there anything you can remember here? Did you ever see a man in a car or truck?"

My brother blurted, "Yea! The first time, when we took everything. He saw me first and he was coming up the hill. Don't remember what he looked like, but we got out of here quick."

"Mike," the officer leaned over and continued in a soft voice, "anything that scares you a lot up here?"

"Yeah! The well! I get chills when I go near it!"

"Okay, people. You can go home now. We'll take it from here." When we left to go home, there were cops everywhere.

Part VIII
A Good Visit

We handed over the items to the police. They said they were going to analyze them and that they may have been used in a crime.

A few weeks went by. The old man stopped coming. The noises ceased. Then, one morning I was awakened by a hand softly touching my shoulder.

I turned over and the old man was smiling a bit. He just looked for a long time, then he said, "We're almost home."

It was a good visit.

Part IX
A Strange Connection

I was thirteen when things began to feel somewhat "normal." I still awoke at 1:00 a.m., made sure my toy chest and the closet door were closed, and made a round in the house with my dog Ziggy, but there were no more noises, footsteps, or appearances. I felt different.

One day I was walking along the banks of Lake Murray staring at the water and admiring the trout tapping the surface of the water for flies and mosquitos. I guess I was pretty mesmerized by what I was observing because I didn't see the elderly gentleman sitting on a rock almost until the last second before I tripped and ran into the huge granite boulder he was perched upon.

He didn't seem to notice me at all. In fact, he looked deep in prayer; concentrating on "something." He was looking out upon the water mumbling in a strange language. He looked, well, like an Indian, dressed in a leather shirt with beads, wearing Levis, and a band around his forehead. He looked in his seventies, eighties maybe. He had a long, gray ponytail, and he sat cross-legged on the rock, hands folded in his lap.

I started to go around the rock so as not to disturb him. As I started to pass him and he was just out of my peripheral vision, I heard him suddenly say, "Thank you, son. You helped McGurdy keep his promise to us. He was a dear friend to all of us. You are blessed. The Great Spirit worked through you. Your grandmother has taught you well. He will soon be at peace."

I didn't even look up, but as he stopped talking I did. I turned around and the gentleman was walking up the hill. He never looked back. A strange connection it was.

Part X
Case Solved

A week after I had my experiences at the lake, I was sitting in the living room watching the Charger game on TV with my dad. There was a knock on the door. It was the police again.

"Mr. Dixon, we need to ask Mike some more questions." My dad nodded in agreement. "Yes, sir."

I snapped to attention.

"Mike, can you remember anything else? Tell us about the well again."

"I get scared like there is something down there."

We went back up to the McGurdy place on Monday. There were more police, a special rescue squad, and forensics people. They lowered a guy down the well. Within two minutes we heard him shout. "Got something! A skull, bones."

There was a perfectly round hole in the back of the skull. The ribs showed several cracks in succession on two ribs. It was horrific! I couldn't believe it. But as soon as they found the skeleton, I felt a huge sigh of relief. We drove back to the house. My dad reached for the phone on the wall and got it by the third ring. "Hello. Yes. Oh my God. What? Yes, we will…Right away."

When my dad hung up the phone he just stared at me. Then he said, "We have to go to the police station."

When we got to the La Mesa Police headquarters we were met by FBI agents, sheriffs, and several others. A captain stepped forward and summed everything up, "Ballistics had found the gun used to murder someone. It fit the skull wound. And the rib damage was the result of a knife wound. A money trail had been under investigation for a year and it led to a businessman in Florida, who had been brought up on tax evasion charges. And it just so happened that he was John McGurdy II, alias Hal Smith.

Your brother Don reported an elderly man in an old rambler had been seen several times at the house over the years. Well, he was smart enough to get the license plate number. We contacted the guy. He lives on the Cuyamaca Reservation. He told us his family members were friends of the McGurdys. He also had a letter from one of McGurdy's daughters explaining how her brother tried to get their father to loan him money but the old man wouldn't do it. The letter went on to explain how she feared for her father's life and that John Jr. would point a .22 caliber pistol at his father and threaten him when he was younger. It had been given to him as a Christmas present from his dad!

The old guy never told anyone but had come up and checked the house, keeping the family's promise. He checked last year and his daughter found the letter and gave it to the sheriff. So, forensics was able to connect the gun, the knife, and the shirt to McGurdy Sr.

Records showed a woman had forged signatures years ago to obtain money in a San Diego Bank account, the McGurdy Estate. Someone didn't ask the right questions.

Jong McGurdy Jr. was charged with the murder of his father, John McGurdy. He confessed and was brought back to San Diego to stand trial. Mrs. McGurdy's body was never found.

John McGurdy Jr. died in prison in 1998, after being sentenced to life. Case closed."

Part XI
Cowles Mountain Today

It is majestic, rising 736 feet above sea level and overlooking a grown San Diego county! It keeps watch on everything from the Cuyamaca Mountains to Pt. Loma, La Jolla and all the way to Tijuana. It is now part of a state park with millions visiting it yearly and ascending its peak. At the foot of Cowles Mountain, just off the trail, there is a sunken wooden post—the last remnants of the barn. Everything, all but gone, except the well! It is a water tower now. It sits behind a strip mall and a restaurant close to the Mission Trails Golf Course at Mission Trails Park.

Every year you can see several Kumayay and Cuyamaca Native Americans scaling the rugged trails on the east side of the mountain. They come in honor of their people. They bring the Great Spirit.

Me? I put flowers at the base of the water tower, say a prayer, and think of my grandma.

Epilogue

Never doubt the power of the soul, the spirit, the sixth sense. Pay attention to who you are and where you come from. And always believe!

For the McGurdys—first pioneers of San Diego
August 14, 2016

Author Biography

Mike Dixon has an interesting background. He is an aspiring baseball player turned jockey, Mike also spent six years in the Navy as a Russian linguist. He has spent the last 40 years teaching Spanish and Russian and coaching football and baseball at various schools throughout California. Mike retired from teaching last year and is currently working in a part-time role at Moss Landing and is the pitching coach at Gavilan Community College. He and his wife Leonor reside in Prunedale, California.

www.ingramcontent.com/pod-product-compliance
Lightning Source LLC
Chambersburg PA
CBHW031417120626
46545CB00006B/2157